Positive Parenting

2-in-1 Value Bundle

Parenting with Purpose & Mindful Habits for Better Parents – The Essential Guide to Disciplining with Empathy and Raising an Emotionally Intelligent Child for First-Time Parents

Aileen Jarvis & Rowan Roffe

professional advice. The content within this book has been derived from various sources. Please consult a licensed professional before attempting any techniques outlined in this book.

By reading this document, the reader agrees that under no circumstances is the author responsible for any losses, direct or indirect, that are incurred as a result of the use of information contained within this document, including, but not limited to, errors, omissions, or inaccuracies.

Table of Contents

Parenting with Purpose

A Practical Guide to Disciplining with Empathy and Raising an Emotionally Intelligent Child

Aileen Jarvis & Rowan Roffe

A FREE GIFT TO OUR READERS

As a way of saying thank you for your purchase, we're offering our readers exclusive access to the bonus content that will help you parent with more confidence and build a stronger relationship with your children TODAY!

Visit this link: https://tinyurl.com/PWP-freegift

or scan QR code:

Introduction

"*It is easier to build strong children than to repair broken men.*" - Frederick Douglass

Historically, children were seen as smaller adults or at least a version of them. It wasn't until Jean Piaget decided to think otherwise and categorize them differently that this mindset changed (Mcleod, 2018). Piaget worked as a translator for the Binet Institute in the 1920s. His job was to translate English versions of questions into French. The questions usually required logical thinking to answer. Piaget was intrigued with the incorrect answers that came from children. This made him curious to pick apart the differences between the thinking of an adult and a child. This is what laid the foundation for his cognitive-developmental theory.

According to Albert Einstein, this discovery was so easy that only a genius could have thought of it.

Today, psychologists address a child's psyche as a complex and unique field of study. Increased focus is put on whether early childhood experiences play any role in cognitive development and behavior or not. Experts are also interested in determining whether nature or nurture has a key role in all this.

Since early childhood is such an important phase of one's life, the experiences one goes through are worthy of the attention and scrutiny they get. There are a hundred and more things that influence the behavior of a child, such as their surroundings, people around them, how toxic or healthy the relationships they are exposed to are, etc. All of these influences are what develop habits, some of which are everlasting.

Then, as the child grows, a set of whole new influences is introduced, which includes self-esteem, social pressures, and school. These, too, contribute to the making of an adult and determine whether the child will grow up into a happy, productive, fulfilled adult.

However, cognitive development starts much earlier. At birth, the size of a newborn's brain is a quarter that of an average-sized adult's. It grows double in size by the time the kid turns one. By the time they hit three, 80% of the brain is already developed, and by the time they turn five, the brain is nearly all grown.

So, your child is grown intellectually by the time they start nursery school. Did you know that a newborn is born with all the neurons (brain cells) it will have for the rest of its life? So that should mean that nurture has a very small part to play, right? To some extent, yes, however, it is the connections between these brain cells that make the difference. These brain connections are responsible for our movement, communication, and thinking. In the first few years of our lives, at least 1 million new synapses (neural connections) are developed per second.

Different regions of the brain are assigned different responsibilities and possess different abilities. Each of these regions develops at different stages throughout childhood, which is why we notice the child learning and making sense of things gradually and not at once. For instance, a kid may not have the cognitive ability to understand why they shouldn't lie. However, when they see the consequences of their lie, they tend to avoid developing the habit. This is because the connections in the brain begin to link with one another and do so in complex ways.

Another thing to note is that the brain's capacity to learn new things declines with age. In layman's terms, the brain is most elastic during early childhood. It has the ability to accommodate various interactions and environments. However, as it matures, it becomes less flexible and more fixated on ideas and behaviors that have already been learned. This is one reason why we fear facing new challenges or unexpected outcomes such as a test score or giving up on a bad habit as novelty and unpredictability take an energy toll on our brain, and our brain's default mode of function is to conserve energy.

Moreover, aging can cause a decline in brain plasticity. When a child reaches the age of one, they begin to differentiate, understand, and mimic sounds and languages. As they grow older, their ability to learn new sounds and languages often slows down. This is because during early development, babies and very young children form neuron connections at a rapid pace. Hence, their ability to learn a new language is much faster and better than adults. We can still learn new languages later in life; however, it becomes more challenging to learn new things, because as the brain develops, the brain becomes more specialized and focuses more on strengthening the neural pathways that already exist.

That being said, the early stages of a child's development are the best times to instill lifelong habits. It is the best time to teach them the difference between good and bad, communicate about rewards and consequences, build their self-esteem and confidence, and raise them to be responsible, emotionally-intelligent, and empathetic adults.

To do this, it is imperative that the majority of the interactions they have with their parents, siblings, and caregivers are meaningful. Kids mimic the behaviors of others. Since they are only making sense of the world around them, they rely on the behaviors, language, and actions of those around them. Therefore, as parents, it is on us to create healthy relationships around our children, be responsive to their needs, address their queries, and allow them to explore and experience things on their own.

But what is a habit? A habit is anything that an individual projects as a natural behavior. It is an automatic response to situations. Think of it as a behavior that manifests itself without any guidance or provocation. According to one research study, children form habits by the age of nine. This leaves parents with a small bracket to act their wisest and instill habits that they want their kids to have and also avoid drilling the ones they don't want. The earlier we begin with healthy habits, the more likely they will stick with them for life.

Most of the time, parents think that it is too early to teach kids important habits. They postpone it until the child is able to start understanding them. This is a result of underestimating the potential of kids. For instance, take cleaning the room as an example. If the child sees you putting the toys aside to one side of the room or say, in a toy basket every time they are done playing with them, they too, will pick it up when they learn to crawl or walk. If you lead by example, they will eventually get the hang of it. A simple habit as such can have a significant impact on the kid's life as it teaches them organization and management. You will ultimately want them to clean their room when they are old enough to do so. Imagine if you start today, you can save yourself from all that nagging and complaining and disciplining them. It sounds like a good bet, doesn't it?

This is what this book is about. It focuses on parenting with purpose – a concept that revolves around intentional mindfulness. What exactly does this mean, however? Parenting with purpose is about building connections that will be defining for the child-parent relationship in the years to come. It puts a strong emphasis on communication, setting attainable and age-appropriate goals for kids, and providing positive reinforcement to help youngsters achieve to the best of their abilities.

Everything we do as parents will be a calculated and cautious step in the right direction. We will learn how to raise well-behaved, conscientious, and disciplined children. We shall discuss the many obstacles parents face when raising a child, numerous challenges such as public tantrums, resisting change, outbursts, or being disobedient. We will talk about the mindset kids usually have and focus on the reasons as to why they can be a handful at times. And while we're at it, we'll look at many actionable steps to overcome the challenges of parenthood and form a stronger bond with our kids – one that isn't forced, one-sided, or difficult. A focus on communication and effective upbringing techniques (positive reinforcement approaches) tends to stimulate kids to develop to the best of their abilities. The book outlines these techniques and provides actionable tips for handling common situations and crises.

What makes this a unique guide is that most of the work and studies mentioned have scientific backing and stem from personal experiences, too. If you follow the strategies and techniques to raise an aware and disciplined child, your life as a parent will be less stressful and more rewarding.

But why should you listen to us?

Real-world knowledge based on experience – that's what we, Aileen Jarvis and Rowan Roffe, have to offer. Our duo has an extensive background in child development work. As specialists and coaches, we have faced the daily struggles of parents and worked together with them to enhance communication and help kids grow up healthy and responsible.

Today, we dedicate our time to creating books about parenting and make it easier for new parents to raise sensible and responsible kids. All of the information is sourced from the actual work that we have done with the many parents that turned to us for advice.

Apart from being professionals in the field of child development, we also derive inspiration from our own families. As parents to two and three children, respectively, we have many personal examples to share and help empower other parents.

Chapter 1: Parenting with Purpose? Wait... What?

You must have had one of those days where you wished things were different. The little one comes crying to you for having stuck a peanut in their nostrils, having misplaced their hat, which obviously they are wearing, or because they wanted to play in the snow when it's 40 degrees outside. You find play-doh stuck on your favorite rug, jam on your new shirt, and lipstick marks on the walls. Yes, we all have had those days, and the worst part, this doesn't stop there. The absurdities continue to grow with every passing day, leaving you wishing for a time machine.

But you also can't forget the moment you held them in your hands for the first time, and they smiled back at you. Wasn't that beautiful too? You knew, at that moment, there can be nothing more beautiful than this.

Parenting isn't easy. It wasn't supposed to be! And we say this because we have had dozens of parents come to us to discuss the not-so-good habits of their kids and try to make sense of that behavior. We get it. You want the best for your children. You want them to rise up to their true potential, have strong personalities, be empathetic towards others, be emotionally-intelligent, and well-behaved. You want them to do good in school, learn compassion, have meaningful relationships, be noble, and be disciplined as opposed to throwing tantrums all over the place, questioning your ability as a parent.

But what if, in one sane moment, you see things from their perspectives. Are they really wrong? Would you not have done the same had you been in their shoes? You made them sit in their car seat forcefully and then bribed them with ice cream on the way back if they stayed quiet and behaved well. What else would you expect from a kid who doesn't understand the concept of promises yet?

Here's where we, as parents, are erroneous. We are trying to raise them using submission rather than giving them a purpose to change their behavior or actions for good. Parenting with purpose is about nurturing and empowering your child in a non-violent manner that offers guidance and recognition. It is also about setting some boundaries, rewarding good behavior, and reprimanding negative ones using mindful intentions instead of punishment.

It entails leading by example, being a teacher and mentor, showing care, being sensitive towards their needs, offering consistent support and bouts of motivation, encouraging them to be independent, providing affection and emotional security, helping them differentiate between positive and negative habits, making room for healthy communication, rewarding small accomplishments, supporting their best interests, and demonstrating empathy.

Speaking at a lecture on the Origins of Human Cooperation, psychologist Michael Tomasello stated that:

> *From when they first begin to walk and talk and become truly cultural beings, young human children are naturally cooperative and helpful in many—though obviously not all—situations. And they do not get this from adults; it comes naturally. (Tomasello, 2008)*

If that is true, our job is basically half done. They already have the potential to distinguish right from wrong. We just need to provide them with the right situations. This is the goal of parenting with purpose—offering the child guidance so that they move in the right direction. It improves communication as well as the mutual bond between you and your child. It allows you to teach them the right values, comprehend where they are coming from, and set attainable goals for them to excel in.

That included, there are many perks to parenting with purpose. For starters, it helps your kid to have a stronger bond with you. The parent and child relationship shapes the personality of the kid, predicts behavior, and gives an insight into their choices and interests. Many studies focus on the health benefits of a strong parent and child bond (Moore, Kinghorn, & Bandy, 2011).

It is a no-brainer that loving parents raise loving kids. The type of engagement you have with your child is what will determine the type of responses and interactions they will have. It also determines the quality of their emotional and social health. Children who are raised by loving and devoted parents are more likely to create the similar bonds with others as they grow older. Their relationships tend to be more meaningful and fulfilling as opposed to someone who has grown up seeing their parents fight all the time. A child that is able to express their emotions with their parents without feeling hesitant has a better chance of dealing with their problems independently and regulates their emotions better.

There are several other benefits of having a strong parent-child relationship.

- It promotes the linguistic, mental, and cognitive development of the child.
- It leads to better social skills.
- It builds better academic skills.
- Healthy parent involvement allows children to exhibit confident and optimistic social behavior.
- It promotes the adoption of healthier habits in general.
- Children feel more driven and motivated to power through the various challenges they face.
- It helps them build strong problem-solving skills as they know they can always turn to someone for help.

Following that, you might be wondering how to go about strengthening your relationship with your little one, right? Here are some great examples to get you started on the right foot.

Start Early: You must have heard how they say that the moment a woman discovers that she is expecting, she forms a bond with her unborn right from that moment. On the other hand, fathers become fathers the moment they hold their newborn in their arms. Research shows that fathers who are more involved in the lives of their kids during the early years share a stronger bond with them as they grow (Sarkadi, Kristiansson, Oberklaid, & Bremberg, 2007). Thus, the #1 rule to strengthening the bond and parenting them with a purpose in mind is to be there for them.

Prioritize Them Above All: Your involvement and interaction with your child should be your top priority today and forever. Kids are quick to pick up the behaviors they see around them and form connections too. Someone who seems to care little will eventually experience the same distance from the child when they grow up. Therefore, show them how much you care and love them with your actions. Spend quality time with them, invest in their health and well-being, show concern about their little problems, and hear them out when they come to you seeking help. Instead of trying to fit them in your busy schedule, how about fitting your other commitments in a schedule that revolves around them for starters?

Be Present: Kids are little explorers. They are interacting with a million new things every day. They are clearly overwhelmed, thus the never-ending trail of whys and whats. Your goal is to be responsive to their inquisitive needs instead of shushing them away or handing them a tablet to play with so that you can enjoy some quiet time in the house.

Understandably, there may be some tough days, and you are facing some bigger battles in your mind, but telling a child "no" is one of the biggest mistakes you can make as a parent. This shows disinterest and a lack of care. They will feel unheard and devalued. Be attentive, communicate, visualize, and see things from their perspective to sense the wonderment they are experiencing.

Empathize: It is pivotal that you, as a parent, allow your kids to show and express their emotions openly. Don't suppress them or tell them to "toughen up" when they are on the verge of crying. Instead, allow them to vent their emotion out. Help them project their emotions in the right way and start talking about how to deal with them when they feel overwhelmed. This can be the start of developing emotional intelligence in your child. This way, they will learn to be more empathetic and differentiate between different sets of emotions and how to deal with them.

Be Communicative: Be open to talk about things, even the smallest things, to show your child that they have someone they can come to. The mode of communication should be supportive, friendly, and caring. However, if you want them to learn discipline from an early age, make it a habit to lay some ground rules and expectations. For instance, you can expect them to address you or any other elder in the house with respect, be open to a difference in opinion, listen to the advice given, and act accordingly. You shouldn't allow them to take advantage of your gentleness or push your buttons.

Establish Trust: Trust is the most important cornerstone of every relationship. Your kid should be able to rely on you for advice and support and feel secure. Keep in mind that this level of trust will not be established with false promises, shattering their confidence, or by invading their privacy. It is advisable to keep a check on them as their social interactions widen so they don't fall into bad company.

Be Involved: Show your interest and involvement in the things they are doing. If they are in school, show an interest in their friends, academia, and relationships. Keep in touch with their teachers and caregivers to know how they are doing.

Be an Active Listener: Show your interest with more than a hmm or ok. Sometimes, kids come to us with valuable concerns and information, which we bluntly disregard, thinking they are too young to be discussing them. For instance, we once had a family visit us where the 6-year-old had stopped talking altogether. In the past, the girl seemed fine and responded to all our questions with engaging answers. However, during the recent visit, she wasn't initiating conversation and seemed less inquisitive. As it turned out, we found out later that she was being bullied at school repeatedly. She had been shushed by her father and told to act strong. The parents were too busy to do anything about it, and she was too weak to take matters into her own hands. So she was dealing with it all independently, which was clearly affecting her health and performance at school.

The point is, children may not be able to communicate like adults due to a limited vocabulary, but they do show some signs of distress and worry. As their primary caregiver, it is your job to notice them, probe, and listen to them.

Show Respect: Respect is another touchy subject with kids. Although they are tiny, they still have high self-esteem and want to be treated like adults. Have they not asked for the same snacks you eat or the beverages you drink? Have they not thrown a tantrum over why daddy gets to drink the red juice in the wine glass, and they are stuck with milk in a bottle? Children like being acknowledged. They want to feel valued. They want their opinions to be heard and appreciated. They demand respect for their thoughts, beliefs, and ideas. Failing to offer them that makes you a bad parent in their eyes.

Boost their Ego: Encourage them when they are giving their 100% to something, even if they are failing at it. The goal is to motivate them to not give up and continue trying.

Children need recognition as much as adults. Imagine how you would feel if someone else other than yourself gets appreciated for the work you did. Would you not feel disheartened? Your kid will feel the same if they sense their efforts aren't being appreciated. Encouragement helps boost their self-esteem and confidence. Criticism should be kept to a minimum and only expressed when the child deliberately repeats the same mistakes over and over again. Show them that their actions and effort are valued.

Parenting with purpose allows parents to discover the child's strengths and talents. Believe it or not, parents are better detectives than Sherlock Holmes. In fact, if Sherlock Holmes and Parents are ever made to compete against one another, parents will win by a large margin. After all, they have become good at spotting the tired eyes of their toddlers, the unnecessary crying before bedtime, tantrums before they even began, and suspicious noises from the room of their teenage son/daughter. Therefore, when it comes to discovering a child's true talents and skills and nurturing them, parents serve as the most important asset.

A renowned parenting expert, Nikki Bush, suggests that parents are possibly the only ones that can spot the hidden talents and skills their kids possess. They also are the only ones that can nurture them without putting any pressure on the kid.

There are great advantages of recognizing a talent right in the bud. The earlier it is noticed, the greater the chances of its developing into a full-fledged skill learned over the years via practice. The first twelve years, according to Dr. Bush, are the most crucial in uncovering true talents and skills in children.

The simplest way is to observe what activities excite or bore the child. This can be done in a number of different ways, such as:

Exposing Them to a Variety of Activities: A lot of times, parents have a set number of expectations from their kids. Some parents deliberately try to impose certain ideas on their kids. For example, wanting them to be a doctor when they grow up as everyone else in the family is one. Why is this wrong? It is because you are fixating their brain onto just one of the million other ideas. Just because you are familiar with it and it seems like a good and reputable option in the future doesn't mean your kid will want that too. Therefore, let them be the judge and jury of what they want to spend their time doing. Expose them to numerous activities and see what their heart is set on. Sometimes, the gifts we have aren't transmitted into our kids. Thinking they would naturally choose what you chose because it's in the genes stops kids from recognizing their true potential until it's too late.

Exposure to a variety of things is the best way to discover their strengths and interests.

Paying Attention: Once the child has been exposed to a set of different things, notice what activities they find most intriguing. The activities they enjoy will be repeated several times. That makes it easier to know what they have fallen in love with. While paying attention and observing their interests, encourage them to continue with them without forcing them to try new ones. Talent may be an intrinsic trait, but it requires practice and repetition to be polished. Therefore, aim for that. If they love doing something more often, maybe that is what they want to be doing when they grow up.

Inquire about Their Interests: One of the easiest things you can do is ask. They are clearly the happiest when conversed with about the things they like. It can serve as a great bonding time for both the parent and the child. Children are storytellers. All you need to do is push them a little to open up. Talking about the things they enjoy doing or want to do more of is a great conversation starter. Ask them what comes naturally to them and how do they want to spend their time.

Letting them Lead: While exposing them to different activities, try to let them be the ones to pick. One way to do so is by giving them a few choices. For instance, ask them if they would like to play outside, do coloring or play the piano. These activities can be substituted with things they usually like. The thing that they choose will be the one they are most interested in. The idea is to let them lead so that they pick the things that come naturally to them. You will just be a guide or coach. You can offer some suggestions to help them choose but be sure to encourage them to decide themselves. This will also teach them to rely on their own emotions and make their interests a priority.

Encouraging Them Despite How Unrealistic It Seems: Sometimes, the interests they pick may be stupid. They aren't as big as you to weigh the pros and cons of everything. However, instead of discouraging, stopping them, or laughing at them for choosing poorly, encourage them. If they say they want to fly a plane, tell them that they can. Don't discourage their dreams. If they have a knack for airplanes, tell them that they can fly one once they know all the instructions and manuals. Sit with them and discuss the many different parts they should know about the procedure of flying a plane, how to pack for a flight, etc. The goal is not to squash their big dreams and instead encourage them throughout.

Staying Attuned: Children are naïve creatures. They don't know when to stop talking, so chances are they are going to be talking about their interests more than once. You just have to be a vigilant listener. Even when they are talking about things that don't interest you or stories you have already heard 10+ times, listen. Give them the attention and curiosity they require. At the same time, also pay attention to the things they don't like. For instance, if they keep telling you how they don't like to ride a bike and instead would like to go to ballet school, notice that too. These are also subtle clues that will come in handy when shaping their personalities. Also, you will avoid pushing them into doing things when you know they are disinterested.

Being Ok With the Switching: Tell us that your child has not once embarrassed you in front of everyone by doing something they absolutely hated doing before. You just told everyone how they don't like coconut cookies, and there is your little one gulping down one after the other, only making you seem like a stupid and inattentive parent. Changes of heart happen. Even adults experience it. Your child might like something one day and have a complete change of heart towards it the next. Even when they seem to excel at something, if they seem disinterested, let it go. Excellence doesn't equate to passion. It is okay for them to quit something. As a parent, we have to learn to be okay with it. It is not the end of the world. They are just exploring their options. They still have a long way to go before deciding on something. Let them be!

Parenting with purpose helps parents raise emotionally-fulfilled and empowered children.

What does emotionally-fulfilled even mean?

Emotional fulfillment refers to a state of being satisfied with who you are and being ok with it. It is about being content with your success as well as failures and accepting yourself for who you are. How can parenting with purpose achieve that?

It allows kids to embrace their greatness and believe in their potential. It helps them learn discipline and how to stay composed and dedicated. It involves nurturing their abilities and empowering them to be their best. In today's world, there is less emphasis on having good jobs or careers and more on having a fulfilling and rewarding life. This shift in the dynamic is what parenting with purpose aims to achieve.

This shift is only possible with empowerment – a belief to raise a child who feels capable of managing their emotions and actions independently. Empowerment begins with helping the kid discover their strengths, building their confidence, and fostering their resilience when facing challenges. Empowering children from an early age is crucial in helping them learn to deal with the ups and downs of life as well as giving them the inner gusto to pushing themselves towards pursuing their dreams.

If we look at the literal meaning of the term empowerment, it means to put in. It is derived from a Latin word and used to mean to cause power. Therefore, for parents, empowering their children means providing them with the optimum conditions in which they feel powerful and autonomous. The biggest question, however, is how to do that.

Luckily, there are some basic steps to allow them to leave the nest.

Start with responsibilities. Give them a few chores or duties to take care of. Kids love the attention they receive when they are put in charge of something. It makes them feel important and valued. Giving them responsibilities and acknowledging their contribution to the task makes them feel accomplished and boosts their confidence. This sense of responsibility and improved confidence will serve as a foundation for them to deal with future obstacles.

Next, you can celebrate their accomplishments, no matter how small they are. This demonstrates that the work they did was indeed something, and they feel they contributed in some beneficial way. You don't always have to make a big gesture like taking them out for ice-cream or allowing them another hour on the tablet. The celebration can be as simple as making their favorite dish for dinner or letting them pick out a movie of their choice. The objective is to show them that their accomplished work holds value. This positive reinforcement will encourage them to do more and take on new challenges – thus empowering them.

Third, keep guiding them and supporting them throughout their journey. Don't just rush to their help when you foresee a problem. Let them use their brains and the limited resources they have to handle it themselves. Helping them out every time they hit a roadblock will teach them to become reliant. As parenting experts, we believe this discourages the child from taking on the challenges and decreases confidence in their capabilities. You want them to think that they can figure out a solution on their own.

Parenting with purpose isn't about punishment but rather a stimulating approach to help children power through challenges independently.

Continuing from the point before, one of the reasons kids find it difficult to take control of things is because they fear judgment and punishments. When you opt for purposeful parenting, you don't rely on such old-age methodologies to get the job done. Instead, you choose to be more open about the concerns and problems the kids are facing and help them navigate their problems. This isn't about pulling them down but rather building them from the ground up. You help them deal with the challenges without taking the power away from them. They still think that they are in charge and feel more driven to work things out as the fear of punishment or judgment is eliminated. The children know that even if they fail, they will not be put down, compared with other kids their age, or punished for failing. That makes them feel more confident from the beginning.

To do so, parents need to teach their kids coping skills to get through any difficulty they face. Coping skills allow children to make sense of the problem and address it without losing their temper. Children with stress coping skills grow up to be more self-reliant, confident, and mentally-healthy.

Let them know that the problems they face are nothing but opportunities to learn from and grow. Tell them that there are two ways to look at a problem. One is from a negative point of view. Those with a negative mindset easily give up when faced with a challenge or constantly complain about how difficult and unfair it is. Conversely, the second way to look at a roadblock is with positivity. You don't see the problem as a problem but rather a challenge you need to overcome. You also acknowledge the fact that even if you fail at it, it will still be worth attempting and leave you with a valuable lesson. When kids begin to see obstacles as opportunities and challenges, they put in more effort to overcome them.

Lead by Example: Children do many things, and one of those is observing. No matter how many times you teach them, they are still going to follow the actions and behaviors you exhibit in times of stress. If you tend to lose your cool, sulk or whine, so will they. If you get angry and start cursing or throwing things, so will they. The point is, what sort of example are you going to set for them to mimic? Therefore, be a role model and demonstrate a positive and uplifting attitude when faced with a problem. Don't throw in the towel and give up, because your child will too!

Failing isn't that bad either.

Most importantly, let them know that it isn't the end of the world if they fail. Failing is a blessing in disguise as it introduces children to some new emotions such as fear, rage, anger, jealousy, nervousness, etc. It is also important to learn how to cope with them when they become too overpowering. Luckily, parenting with purpose also gives children the chance to experience these emotions and cope with them. We will discuss more on how to teach your children to handle "big emotion" later in this book.

Finally, parenting with purpose lays the foundation for mutual respect between the child and the parent. As parents, we need to understand that in order to be respected, we have to give respect. This isn't a one-sided thing. Kids need a reason to respect you, and since they are masters of mimicking from an early age, the easiest way to build a mutually respectful relationship with them is by reciprocating the same.

It isn't uncommon for us to deal with inquiries about how to discipline kids when they are disrespectful and don't abide by the rules parents have set for them.

Disrespect isn't something intrinsic. Kids aren't born with it. It is something we nurture in them through the environment and sometimes through our parenting mistakes. Although we shall discuss this more in chapter 3, the type of parenting styles you have explains a lot about the behavior of a child.

As parenting experts, we know how frustrating it can be to live with an undisciplined toddler or teenager. You feel like nothing you say is acknowledged or considered important. You might even feel like a complete failure at times. You must have had those days where you felt extremely embarrassed or guilty about the way your kid acted out in front of everyone. How they walked right past you. How they didn't pay any heed to your concerns, how they turned a blind eye to you, how they responded with cussing or whining to one of your requests, how they hit you in the face out of anger, how they used bad words to get back at you at a family gathering, etc. These aren't just words, but actual concerns we have addressed.

What we think is that, as parents, it is our duty to teach our kids how to act in a civilized society. It is our job to tell them not to talk back, present themselves in a civilized way, be empathetic towards others, show gratitude towards elders, and more. However, the manner in which we choose to teach them these pivotal behavioral milestones is what makes all the difference.

As stated before, parenting with purpose doesn't rely on punishment-based methods to discipline the kids.

This is where mutual respect comes in. So how do you treat them when they throw a public tantrum, take off their shoes, hit you, and push you in a busy grocery store only because you said no to their favorite candy?

With mutual respect, period.

Mutual respect minimizes the chances of conflicts and the animosity resulting from it during family tensions. On the one hand, parents should respect the age-appropriate choices of their kids and the values they hold and refrain from imposing their own age-appropriate ideas on them or losing their temper. On the other, kids should respect the authority which parents hold and not use harsh words to express their anger or angst. There are numerous benefits of mutual respect between both parties.

For instance, mutual respect promotes equality. Parents avoid using their authoritative position in the home to dictate the choices of their kids despite knowing more. Children, especially when they are going through the teen ages, experience swift mood changes. They want to be more in control of their decisions or at least included in major ones about their lives. Too much involvement by the parent can make them feel caged and, thus, unhappy. Creating spaces where mutual respect prevails from and for both the parties is the foundation to improve and strengthen existing relationships. Mutual respect establishes a healthy family environment for both parents and children where communication is kinder, and interactions are looked forward to.

Secondly, homes, where mutual respect is considered a priority, tend to be closer and more fused. According to Larry Nelson, children who feel respected by their siblings and parents have stronger bonds with them, even when they move out. This is especially true for dads who promote mutual respect in the house. The kids also tend to have higher self-esteem and self-worth than those who feel unheard or dictated. Showing respect is telling them that their privacy and independence are acknowledged.

It also serves as a great means to resolve any conflicts of opinions or ideas in the house and keeps it peaceful. It is the fastest way to resolve issues. Picture this: your child has committed a blunder that has left you disappointed gravely. You want to lash out, give them a piece of your mind, and discourage them from repeating the behavior again. However, instead of doing that, you politely ask them what made them act that way and whether something bothered them or had them stressed out.

The child, in this situation, instead of feeling opposed, belittled, or discouraged, will feel valued and cared for. They will see that they are accepted and loved despite the mistakes they made and that the parent isn't angry but rather more worried. The chances of them opening up and talking about why they did what they did and whether it was intentional or not are higher. The first step to any conflict resolution is the acknowledgment that there exists a problem and second involves talking about it to find a solution together.

This form of parenting style accomplishes both and thus results in its resolution. Mutual respect allows both the parent and the child to express their concerns and feelings without sounding harsh or judgmental. Another example can be your daughter wanting to go for a sleepover at a friend's. Instead of rejecting the idea outright, let her know that you don't like the idea but trust their judgment to make the right choice.

Lastly, mutual respect promotes healthy communication between the child and the parent. One way of showing mutual respect is by becoming an active listener and hearing out the things that bother your child or cause them stress. This way, the children feel that they are heard and cared for. Another way of showing respect is asking for forgiveness over rude behavior, invasion of privacy, or nagging – even if it is done by the parent. When forgiveness is sought by the parent, it lets your child know that even their role models can sometimes do flawed things. This makes communications healthier as the child won't feel ignored and know that they can always turn to their parents for advice.

Some other ideal ways to show respect and avoid power struggles include:

Asking Fewer Questions: As parents, we are often overly-possessive about our kids. We want to know about their day, talk to them on the phone 10 times a day as they head for college, and be an active part of their love and married life when they decide to find someone. Children, on the other hand, not so much. As they grow older, they want to explore and experience things their way.

Firing at them tens of questions at once the moment they come back from school can trigger irritation. Older kids are less inclined to share every single detail about their day. They are least interested when they know the answers will make you judge them or question them further. When they feel judged, they think they are not good enough; thus, a visible decline in their self-esteem is observable.

Let them take control of how and when they want to spill the beans and don't hold it against them if they don't. They are in that phase of life where control makes them feel stronger and more autonomous. Therefore, if you want to show them that you respect them, simmer down the long array of questions. If you are still intrigued and would like to be a part of their lives, let them come to you or choose a better time to bring up the topic casually. You don't want them to feel pushed into telling you things as it takes away their sense of control. Let them manage things at their end, and when they feel ready to come and have a discussion about it, hold your judgments and opinions.

So instead of asking where they had been and why hadn't they picked up your call, tell them that you are so glad that they are finally home and how much you missed having them around.

Show Respect Towards Their Willingness: If they seem disinterested in some activity, stop shoving it in their faces just because you know they will like it. For instance, a parent pressuring the child into trying sushi because they think they will like it is asking them to do something against their will. When the goal is to show respect and not force your children into doing something you want them to do, the way you present the ideas or make suggestions would be different. For instance, when you want your children to try new food, you can ask them if they will be willing to give their taste buds something new to try or talk about how yummy it is. If they still resist, give them their space and don't push.

The same applies to things they like but, for some reason, aren't interested in doing right away. For example, making your kid play the piano in front of everyone or greeting relatives and friends with a hug, even though they express that they don't want to, is an indirect way of undermining your children's choice in refusing to participate in an activity that they are not comfortable with and undermining their autonomy over their own body.

When we use coercion, we not only make the environment uncomfortable for them but also miss out on a great opportunity to show respect towards their choices.

It may not seem like a big thing to you right now, but since the ultimate goal of parenting with purpose is raising well-behaved, emotionally-intelligent, and resilient human beings, we can be aware of the mistakes we made as parents and learn to do better from this day forward.

Waiting Before Responding: Sometimes, we become too eager to answer on behalf of our kids. It is acceptable if you notice that your child is shy around others. Even then, let them have a moment before jumping in to answer on their behalf. Maybe they already had an answer or opinion to share. But since you interrupted in between, you halt the opportunity for them to own their voice. Additionally, when kids realize that their parents are always there to answer for them, they become dependent on it. Another thing that can happen is that the child begins to associate quick answering as normal. So when you don't reply to them instantly or in haste like you did the last three times, they feel frustrated and annoyed. They feel that their inquiry isn't worth discussing or addressing, which further discourages them to initiate conversations with the parent or come to them for help.

So what seems to be the right approach here?

Here's what we tell parents to do instead. Ask a question in return. Confused? Imagine this: one of your neighbors comes up to your kid and asks them how they like the new bike that they got for Christmas. Rather than responding with, "He loves it. He can't get enough of it", try something like, "Hey, do you want to tell her about your new bike and the bell?" Do you notice the difference? Instead of responding on their behalf, you provide them the opportunity to speak for themselves and also subtly let them know what they can talk about.

If they come to you asking questions that boggle them, don't just answer without thinking. Instead, ask about what they think the answer is. For example, your kid asks you if lions run faster than cheetahs or not. Rather than telling them the correct answer, say this: what do you think?

Basically, you are giving them the opportunity to think harder, express their ideas even when they think they are wrong, and be confident while delivering them.

What about situations where there isn't any definitive answer? Aren't those the hardest ones to tackle? Instead of disappointing them right away with an "I don't know", how about lifting their confidence by complimenting them with sentences like, "Wow, I am amazed you thought about it! Someone's growing up too fast and asking all these big kid questions," or, "I am so proud of your little mind that keeps coming up with such interesting questions, good job! Mommy is not sure either. Let's find out together."

The goal is to leave the room open for future conversations. You don't want to shun them away.

Letting Them Enjoy Some Privacy and Space: Parents who hover over their kids obsessively and want to be included in every small conversation and choice are often disliked by the children. The children feel policed and invaded. This is highly common when they are moving into the teen ages. They want to keep things private, but their parents still treat them like toddlers and want to be in their faces 24/7.

We understand how hard it can be for you to maintain some distance as you feel ignored. But this transition will eventually take place. Additionally, you also sometimes try to infuse your touch into their attire or accessories, like putting a barrette into their hair for extra sparkle, adding a muffler to their overcoat, or tucking their shirts into their pants unannounced. It's quite confusing because you used to do the exact same things a year or two ago, and they never seemed to complain. Now, they are all annoyed and growling at you. Why? It is because as kids grow older, they develop a stronger sense of independence. They feel like they have a reputation to uphold as a "grown-up". And doing something like adjusting their hair or pulling down their sweater undermine that sense of autonomy.

These fixes could also be interpreted as an invasion of personal space, and nobody likes that. When we resist making these fixes, we show them that we acknowledge and respect their newly developed autonomy. For example, the next time you see some ketchup on their face, instead of wiping it off with a napkin in front of their friends right away, let them know without embarrassing them that they have ketchup on the corner of their lips and allow them to handle the situation however they want to.

Chapter 2: Inside the Mind of a Child

As discussed in the introductory paragraphs of the book, children aren't the mini versions of adults. The working and functioning of the brain are different. It develops rapidly during the early ages and reaches about 90% of the full-grown adult size by the time the kid starts kindergarten. Therefore, it is essential that we explore these differences and understand its inner workings, how the process of thinking takes place, and what behaviors are expected during that phase. One of the most astonishing things about the human brain is the ability to be curious. Luckily, the urge to explore and expand our knowledge starts at an early age. This is why it will be unfair to not discuss that in detail.

Kids Have a Curious Mind

As humans, we are bombarded with new information every second. However, how much of it do we actually remember or take in? This was the premise of one of the countless studies related to human psychology conducted at the University of California by Charan Ranganath, a psychologist, and the lead researcher. He believes that despite having the curiosity to discover new things, our minds don't really take it all in. To prove this, he asked a few members of the research committee if they recalled the incidents of two days before.

Can you recall the events of the previous week with full accuracy? This curiosity about why we retain some of the knowledge and forget the rest had him intrigued. So he and his colleagues summoned 19 volunteers for an experimental study. Each volunteer was handed a list of 100+ trivia questions. The questions were randomly selected, some about dinosaurs and others about award shows and movies. Ranganath didn't provide the volunteers with the answers and asked the volunteers to rate each question based on how curious they were to find out the answer. Later, they were presented with the list again and asked to view the answer of each on the screen. Before the answer to each question popped up, there was a 14-second gap during which the participants were shown a random photograph of a face. Their response to each question was monitored by an fMRI machine and recorded. The volunteers were then asked to take part in another surprise recognition test where they were asked about how well they recalled the answers as well as the photographs. Ranganath noted that the more curious the volunteers were about questions – as some were quite interesting and other boring – the better their memory. The answers they were most interested in were not the only thing recollected, but the face that preceded it was as well.

To further confirm the hypothesis that curiosity does play a crucial part in learning and memory, the volunteers were called up again for another follow-up study the next day. The same results were received. They were able to recall the answer as well as the face. This proved that when intrigued, the brain was better at learning and creating memories.

Another valuable insight during the studies was that when curiosity was stimulated, the brain experienced an increase in one of its regions that regulated pleasure and reward.

It was also revealed that when curiosity motivates us to learn something new, the hippocampus – the region of the brain responsible for creating new memories – sees increased activity. It is safe to say that curiosity is the one thing that escalates our chances of learning and remembering.

Kids experience the same curiosity. This curiosity is what shapes most of their memory and recall functioning. The more intrigued they are about something, the more likely it is that they will be eager to learn about it and memorize it.

This curiosity is also another reason why there exist power struggles between the parent and the child. The never-ending array of demands, questions, and requests are all backed up by curiosity. Be it them wanting to bathe themselves, know what's inside a marble, or demanding to have ice cream after midnight, these are just some of the many demands a parent has to go through. Any of these demands can instigate an epic show of tantrum if not handled properly.

However, the most important thing to understand here is that they are not deliberately doing all of those things to see you upset. Some are quite age-appropriate because that is what their brain tells them to do.

Understanding the Toddler's Brain

Children need to feel safe. The moment they feel scared or threatened is the moment they shut down.

Social interactions are also not deeply ingrained in the mind of a child. Little ones may often act in an anti-social or an aggressive way because they don't know exactly how to interact with others.

In the middle of a temper tantrum, a child is so overrun by emotions that it becomes virtually impossible to hear you or respond to logical arguments.

The bottom line is this – kids aren't trying to be difficult. Their brain is still not fully developed. They process information in a specific way. You need to modify your approach to make sure you're being heard and understood. Finally, no child is trying to be difficult. There's always a reason for challenging behavior that you need to pinpoint as an adult.

So how can you not lose your sanity and understand things from their perspective? The simplest way is to let them teach you how they are feeling. Take a look at some of the many things kids wish their parents would understand below.

Can you tell me once more?

A lot of the time, as parents, we begin to lose patience when our kids come to us asking the same thing for the fiftieth time in a day. It annoys you to your core, and you just wish there was someplace you could go to, to avoid being questioned about the same thing once again.

However, what you don't realize is that your kid DOES need you to repeat the answer again.

So why shouldn't you be annoyed? As it turns out, the reason we are able to remember, recall, take, and follow instructions is because we adults have well developed executive function skills. Kids, on the other hand, don't.

Let's understand it better with an example. You just told your child that they couldn't sleep late on school days. You know how cranky they can get when missing rest, and you don't want to struggle with them the first thing in the morning today. But they want to stay up late too. Despite telling them not to stay up late, their impulse tells them to. They have two choices: either to obey you or to give in to their impulse. For the kid, they can either sleep late or sleep early because you said so. It is like two ends of a river without a connecting bridge in the middle. Telling your kid once about sleeping early is like placing a thin wooden board between the two shores. You know that it won't hold any weight and will collapse after some time. Every time you remind them or better give them genuine reasons why they shouldn't sleep in late, you are adding one more board over the other, making the bridge stronger.

So you see, the stronger the board, the better the connection between the impulses to either obey or defy. It is about making new connections in the brain with repetition. By repeating the same instructions, you are just building the connection stronger and firming up their memory. They may need to listen to something a hundred times, but eventually, they get it the next time.

This is how you can develop their executive function skills. Keep reminding them to improve their recall and memory and use different and more elaborate methods to answer them. The more reason and details they have, the sooner they will learn from it and do or avoid things you want them to.

I don't know the words to express my feelings or tell you what I want.

Kids may feel overwhelmed or scared but don't know how to let their parents know. They might be facing some abuse or bullying at school or at the hands of someone but not be able to express how they feel or make sense of those disgusting feelings. When their mind is filled with stress and anxiety about something, it becomes harder for them to think straight, and that leads to several mistakes, misbehavior, and crankiness.

If you have a toddler, you would know that no one gets as angry, frustrated, and anxious as them. They experience negative emotions, too, as adults. However, the only difference between them and you is that they don't have the knowledge to channel it.

Whenever we are faced with some negative emotion, we let it sink in, think it through, and distract ourselves with something else so that we may stop thinking about it altogether. Sadly, kids can't do that, and the buildup of frustration, anger, and fear comes out in unexpected ways they don't understand either. Even as adults, we sometimes just give in and cry about our state. So why do we expect our kids not to do the same? Why do we tell them to stop crying when they are sad, stop throwing tantrums when they are mad, or tell them to be brave when they are scared out of their minds?

The regions of their brain that are capable of differentiating between various emotions and how to react to each aren't fully developed, which results in the said confusion. So, when they are faced with something negative, the emotion engulfs them whole.

So how do you go about dealing with the misbehavior and tantrums?

Help them label the emotions they are going through while they are experiencing them. For instance, if they are showing frustration over something, let them know that they are feeling angry, and that is how anger feels. An example can be: You look so mad. You are making that face again where your face turns all red.

This way, you have shown them how anger feels, and the next time they feel the same way, they will be better able to express it. When they do, there are a number of ways you can help them handle it – ways that don't include a tantrum.

Another example can be trying to help them validate what they are going through. The acknowledgment from you makes them feel heard and thus calms them down easily. An example of this can be: Oh honey, I am so sorry you feel this way. Once you calm down, I will give you a hug, and we will talk about it.

Finally, you can try the reflection technique. Reflection techniques encompass mimicking your kid's behavior to get their focus. This technique tends to work better with kids who are older than four years old. For instance, if your kids are whining, you can imitate their facial expressions and tone of voice while maintaining eye contact. When they see you copying them, they will probably pause for a brief moment and look at you. That is when you take a deep breath while maintaining eye contact. Chances are they will continue to repeat your action too, if not visibly, then subconsciously. When they do that, let them know that you hear them and know how they are feeling. Tell them you know how much they wanted that something over which the whole episode of anger is about and how you wish they had gotten it.

I don't want to be difficult, but I just can't help myself.

It seems like the story of every day where, by the time evening sets in, we are done with our child's inquisitive nature. They have asked all the questions they could possibly think of, thrown all the major tantrums, cried their eyes out when taken for a bath, caused a scene in the garden for not letting them fly like the birds, and whatnot. But they notice the frustration on your face, and it makes them sad. If only you knew that they weren't doing it deliberately. They just needed something, so they asked you for it. However, you said no to it, which hurt them. As a result, they cried, became mad, or misbehaved with you. That caused you frustration.

However, what most parents don't realize is that the reason kids keep on making blunder after blunder is because they are just learning something entirely new. It will be a miracle if they get it right the first time. And what is all that frustration? Did you learn to speak in a day? Were you potty-trained the very first time? Did you know the answer to 2+2 the minute you saw it written on the board at kindergarten?

No, right? Had your parents shown this level of frustration in front of you, you would have never been able to learn the things you know about today.

The point is, kids are only learning to be independent. They want to take control of their lives. They want to be able to make decisions themselves and choose to do whatever they feel like doing. So if they tell you that they will get dressed themselves today or take a bath on their own, don't get mad if they make a few mistakes and end up with an unmatched pair of socks or empty the whole bottle of shampoo.

At times, it feels like they are intentionally making things harder for you, but they aren't. The worst thing you can do in such a situation where you catch them drinking water from the toilet is to lose your calm and express your anger. If you look at it from another perspective, the perspective where they were just trying to get some water because they were feeling dehydrated and wanting to fulfill their basic need, this will help you to respond in a more caring and logical manner.

The point is, they don't love making the mess, it just happens. One thing leads to another, and their curiosity gets the best of them.

Like any other person trying out something new, kids need experience and practice to learn. In a way, it is good for you that they are making mistakes as they would then know what to expect from you. The scolding and spanking they get after doing something naughty isn't something they will be looking forward to anytime soon. They need practice and some experimentation to differentiate between right and wrong behavior. They need to know the difference between the actions that end with rewards and actions that end with punishment. But this is only possible with the trial and error method.

Thus, as a parent, it is your job to maintain your cool and continue to remind yourself that your children are in a learning process when you feel the urge to vent out your anger and frustration on them.

When you tell your child to not do something, you hope that the word "no" will discourage them from doing something. However, often this produces the opposite effect, prohibiting your child from doing something often make them more anxious to prove themselves that they can do it. So when you tell them not to try and make their own cereal as you fear they will make a mess, they will become more eager to try and prove that your current hypothesis about them is wrong.

So what can you do when that happens?

Start with taking a deep breath and ask yourself this: is it worth starting a fight over this? Is it worth it to make matters worse and get them all riled up to prove their worthiness? What we want you to do is pick what battles are worth fighting and which ones can be let go. Allow your children to learn from their own experiences is not the end of the world when their safety is not jeopardized. For instance, if they are not in the mood to eat their vegetables today, no need to push them over the edge by trying to force them into eating them. Not only will that ruin their mood, but it will also ruin yours. And who has the job to pick them up and calm them again so that they change into their nightgown without causing drama and making sure they go to sleep on time? Yes, it is no one but you. So are you ready for the extra effort and work you will have to do in order to get them changed and into bed after you just made them mad at the dinner table?

Instead of finding yourself exasperated, keep reminding yourself that this is just a phase, and you won't have to deal with it once they grow up and learn to do things properly.

I don't understand your point.

Imagine this: your toddler is having the biggest meltdown of their lives, and you come at them with explanations on why they shouldn't react this way. What do you expect? Do you expect them to listen to you and calm down? You wish!

If anything, your explanations will further increase the intensity and make things worse for you. How much you wish they would just listen to you. Let's picture it more vividly with an example.

You promised to take them to the park the next day, but something urgent came up, and you couldn't make it in time. By the time you are home, it's already dark, which means no visit to the park today. You come home and find your little one eagerly waiting. They are mentally prepared to go to the park. But you ruin all their plans by saying that we will go tomorrow as it's already dark and there is no point going there now. What comes next is an epic tantrum because you just ruined their whole day of planning and waiting.

They sit on the ground, rub their feet against the floor and make the loudest screams possible, leaving you wondering if they have an amplifier installed in their throat. The more you try to reason with them, the worse it gets.

Yes, we have all been in a similar kind of situation. It is impossible to reason with a child when they aren't in their right mind. Nothing you say will make sense to them because they are in the middle of a tantrum.

So how do you tone it all done and postpone the plan for another day?

Remember this: no logical explanations or rationalization will work. So using the approach where you try to knock some sense into them with some reasonable statements won't work. What will work is the validation of the emotions they are going through. Tell them that you fully understand that they are angry because mommy/daddy has hurt their feelings. Apologize for the mistake you made sincerely, and then once they seem interested in having a conversation about it, tell them what happened and what caused the delay. Let's view it applied in an example.

Parent: I am sorry you feel this way. I know I promised to take you to the store to get you your new bat. You have every right to be angry. I would be too if someone promised me something and then forgot about it. I am really sorry. Will you forgive your mommy/ daddy? You want to know why I had to work late today? I had a big presentation to make. Mr. Andrews called me and said that there was work I needed to get done before leaving the office today. I told him that I had to go home and take my son to get a new bat. You know what he said? He said only I can do the work as I am superman. Do you think your daddy is superman?...

Do you notice how the conversation has turned different? You successfully divert their mind from the thing it's stuck on and onto something that piques their curiosity. That is how you handle a tantrum and let your kid calm down.

I'm not trying to ignore you. I just don't understand what you want me to do!

Here's a fun experiment for you to try. Don't think about a kitten playing with wool. We know you are reading this, but try to not think about the kitten right now. You better not be thinking about it!

Raise your hand if you couldn't not think about the kitten. We know you did because it was impossible not to. This is how the human mind works. Even when we are told not to do something or think about doing it, subconsciously the mind already starts doing it. It is only a matter of seconds before you start doing it too. Here's another example. Imagine you are working late at night. You have had your cup of coffee. You are trying to suppress back sleep because the report needs to be submitted tomorrow, and there are tons of reviewing left. The moment you tell yourself not to think about sleep, your subconscious starts releasing melatonin, and in a minute or two, you find yourself yawning like a kitten. Oops, we again reminded you of the kitten, right?

See, it's impossible to control our thoughts. Although we know of means to control most of our thoughts, our kids don't. So the next time you tell them not to go near the stairs or don't hit your sister, what sticks with them is this: go near the stairs and hit your sister. The elements of "not" and "don't" disappear from their mind, and then the focus on doing the forbidden activity remains. So basically, when you tell them not to do something, you are setting them up for doing exactly that. Statements like these offer the opposite of what you have been trying to prevent them from.

So what do you do?

Stop using confusing sentences that start with no, not, or don't. These pose as double requests which confuse the little ones as they can't differentiate between what you want them to stop doing and what you want them to do instead. Unless you want to set yourself up for frustration, reframe your statements into ones that your kid finds easier to understand.

Below are some ways to say "no" without saying no:

- Instead of "No hitting", say, "We use our words, not our hands."
- Instead of "No whining", say, 'It's hard for me to understand you when you are whining. Please talk to me in your regular voice."

- Instead of "Don't play with mommy's phone," say, "Can mommy have this (an object)? You can have this toy instead."

- Instead of "Don't hit your sibling," say, "I appreciate it when you touch your brother/sister gently."

- Instead of "No cookies," say, "I know you like cookies. You can have a cookie after dinner. Now can you show me how to finish your plate nicely?"

- Instead of "Don't kick the table," say, "Are you hurting your feet kicking the table? Can you show me how you are gentle?"

Chapter 3: Let's Assess Your Parenting Style

We can all agree that there is no such thing as the perfect parent. No matter how hard we try to be an ideal parent, we still fail at times. Many expecting parents reach out to us to talk about the right parenting style and what advice we can give to them so that they don't fail at it. Although we try not to dishearten them, we have to understand that there is no advice we can offer that guarantees success. Of course, there are many techniques, practices, and exercises to improve your chances of being an ideal parent, but still, there are always some things that can go wrong.

It is quite laughable how everyone has some tips to offer that they think helped them raise their kids in an ideal manner. What that does is further confuse us as to what approach is the right one.

The first thing we tell parents is that most of the behaviors and actions we exhibit are from our own childhood and the way we were raised by our parents. No matter how good or bad they were, they still serve as significant parameters. Kids who had a troubled childhood or an uncaring family want to be responsible and involved in their children's lives when they become parents. Children who have had a strong bond with their parents want the same values in their homes when they grow up to become parents. So you see, both the good and bad hold importance. Kids who didn't have enough make sure they give their kids all that is in their power so that they don't have to go through the same struggles as them. We emulate the things our parents did and just add a bit of fine-tuning to it to make it our own style. Know that it is a work in progress, and there is always room for improvement and new practices.

Despite all this, there are some distinctive parenting styles in general that nearly all parents follow. There is always a set of characteristics that draw the line between parents. These are what researchers and child experts label as parenting styles.

If you are someone that is too involved in your kid's life, then researchers view it as attachment parenting. If you are someone that enforces certain rules and disciplinary measures that your kids need to abide by, then your parenting style is authoritative.

But there aren't just two but rather 6 different parenting styles. Surprised, right? Well, you will be further intrigued when we begin to list the characteristics of each. First, three parenting styles were identified by a psychologist, Diane Baumrind, in 1960. She believed that there wasn't just one definitive parenting style and those who thought that were wrong. According to her, parenting was mostly synonymous to controlling. To her, that sounded ugly and disrespectful. She believed that all that the parents do was anything but disrespectful and presented three separate categories to help people understand better. At first, she presented her authoritarian parenting style, which was quite stringent and calculated. Parents who imposed this style were highly disciplined and to some extent, cruel too.

Then there were parents who didn't have a care in the world for what their kids were up to. They were rarely concerned about the kind of education they were getting or how were they being brought up. Diane believed that there had to be a third style too, as her research and surveys with various parents didn't let her believe there were just these two ways. She firmly believed that there had to be something moderate between the two extremes.

Later, after further studies, researchers came down to deriving six different parental controls, aka parenting styles.

Each of these differs from one another and have both pros and cons. In this chapter, we shall discuss these in-depth and learn which parenting style is the best of all.

Self-Analysis: What Parenting Style Do You Have?

Since we live in the world heavily relying on labels, you will notice that some parenting styles are more flattering than others. The names themselves determine the kind of control they exhibit and also if they are the most ideal for your child or not. Take a look at each and see which style of parenting you feel most familiar with. Once you identify that, we will determine if it is the right one for you by learning of its pros and cons. If the cons outweigh the pros, you will know that you need to make some modifications to your parenting style.

The knowledge will help you become a better parent for your kids and help them shape their personalities, actions, and behaviors better.

Authoritative Parenting

Authoritative parenting style, despite its name, has proven to be one of the most decent and well-structured parenting styles as it leaves room for healthy communication between the parent and the child while enforcing discipline. On the one hand, the parent encourages the child to speak up, share their concerns and views without any fear of punishment, and on the other, also has some set boundaries and rules they must follow.

According to Holly Klaassen, the author and editor of The Fussy Baby website, this style of parenting sets high expectations for kids to reach but also tells them how to get there. For instance, a parent might have strict rules about getting homework done but will also be willing to help them with it when they need it.

Examples of Authoritative Parenting

Your child comes home with poor grades. You review their paper and praise them on the things they got right but at the same time, also motivate them to work harder the next time and seek help from you whenever they feel stuck.

Another example can be your little one acting out on the way to the grocery shop. You know that they might throw a tantrum so you tell them to behave themselves and if they behave well, they will have the chance to pick two things for themselves.

Pros

- This style of parenting raises well-behaved and strong-willed children.
- Children know that they will always have someone to look up to and be comforted.
- Kids raised under this parenting style also outperform others in academics and other skills.
- They are easy-going and disciplined.
- They are much happier in general and have higher chances of becoming successful.
- They are emotionally-intelligent and know how to regulate their emotions.
- They also have a high sense of self-esteem and are the most resilient.

Cons

The biggest challenge with this parenting style is the extra parental workload. Although the extra pressure does help the kids do better, it puts a lot of pressure on the parents to set the right expectations. Since most of the expectations stem from personal achievements, parents really have to keep raising the standards themselves first and later expect the same from the kids.

Another drawback is that the rules of the authoritative parenting style need modification from time to time, varying as the kid grows older.

Attachment Parenting

The attachment parenting style involves an excessive obsession with the child. It is basically a child-centric parenting style where the goal of the parents is to ensure the safety and comfort of their child. One can expect an increased physical contact with the child, and it continues even when they are growing older. This is mostly associated with moms who can never get enough of their kids and dread every minute they are not with them. Every inquiry and request is met immediately. Every problem and challenge is attended to. The parent might even co-sleep in the same bed. Common characteristics include soothing, blindly supporting the child, and comforting them so that they feel secure in their environment all the time.

Examples of Attachment Parenting

Picture this: You are attending an important work-related meeting from home via phone, and you hear your child's cry from the next room. Without even thinking for a second, you rush for them, pick them up, and comfort them.

Another example of this can be your toddler wanting to sleep in your bed with your spouse because they feel scared of the monsters under their bed. You gladly let them without even consulting your partner.

Pros

It might seem a bit obsessive on the parent's part, but some recent studies show that kids that grow up under the shadow of attentive and attached parents are more independent when they grow up (Miller & Commons, 2010).

They are also good at channeling their emotions as they have never been told to keep them suppressed. Since they are able to express them without hesitation, it makes them less stressed as they don't have to carry any additional burden of worries with them.

Thirdly, they are also more empathetic in nature as they have received the same from their parents. They know that others need support, guidance, and comfort too, and are willing to offer it whenever required.

Cons

For the parent, attachment parenting can be very time-consuming. Since they tend to coddle the children up close, they don't have enough time left to tend to their own needs.

The other spouse might even begin to feel neglected as the other parent is too possessive about the needs of the child. Moreover, the parent with this style of parenting also has no time for social gatherings with their friends and families, adding to their stress levels. Thus, their health might deteriorate, and they will feel isolated from the world.

Helicopter Parenting

This is similar to attachment parenting but think of it as an upgrade. Like a helicopter, the parents of the child keep hovering over the child to protect them. However, this hovering isn't always required, especially when kids reach the age where they begin to hide things from their parents. This over-indulgence and madness to know everything about their day, who were they with, what did they do, etc. can all seem a bit annoying to the kid. But it isn't all bad or negative. It has many perks too, as parents are quick to take an interest in the lives of their kids and thus are always there to lift their spirits, comfort them and drive them when they feel down or like a failure. Helicopter parenting was first observed in 1966 (Slobin, 2017).

Examples of Helicopter Parenting

An example of helicopter parenting is having a playdate at your home with your child's classmates, setting up all the games, being the referee in them, and managing every other aspect all by yourself.

Another one can be your child failing an aptitude test and you writing a letter to the school, asking them to give your kid another chance.

Pros

One of the reasons helicopter parenting is looked upon as ideal is because it helps parents identify any issues or problems with their kids during the early stages. For example, a kid might be bullied at school but doesn't discuss it with anyone. Uninvolved parents might never discover it themselves; however, helicopter parents might notice the changes in their behaviors, the ups and downs in their moods, the reluctance to go to school, or coming back home with bruises and cuts. These signs, although noticeable, often go unnoticed if the parents are less bothered with their life at school.

During an interview, Laura Hamilton, the author of the book *Parenting to a Degree*, told The Boston Globe that helicopter parenting is one of the reasons why so many kids are able to graduate from college with good grades (Hamilton, 2016). It is the involvement of their parents that keeps pushing them from the back and offers support whenever it is needed and in whichever form – emotional, financial, or physical.

Cons

Sometimes, the same parents come off as too controlling and anxious. They might unintentionally poke their noses too much in the business of the child. The child might feel invasion in their privacy and start to get annoyed with the over-supervision. Moreover, it becomes harder for parents to let go of their kids when they grow older as they fear that if they are not watching over their kids' every step, something bad would happen.

Secondly, parents who hover over their kids 24/7 also give into instant gratification. They are quick to hand over whatever their kid demands and thus make the child think that each request is answerable. This prevents them from developing discipline in their life and face challenges on their own without having their mommy or daddy backing them up. This lack of discipline and extreme reliance on parents can harm their personality. Since everything is handed to them, they rarely win things on their own in their lives.

Uninvolved Parenting

Uninvolved parenting is when a parent chooses not to care, get involved, or is unable to do so due to some reason. For instance, if one of the parents lives abroad, has died, is separated, or working multiple jobs to make ends meet are all reasons why a parent might be able to be as involved with their child and as responsive to their child's needs.

Uninvolved parents have little emotional involvement. They might not know how their child is doing academically, what his/her interests are, what they wish to become when they grow up, what friends their child hangs out with, etc.

The reason this style of parenting is looked down upon by many child experts is that the child feels utterly unappreciated, unheard, and unloved. Some of the most common characteristics of an uninvolved parent include indifference towards their child, inability to access and address their personal needs, an uncaring attitude, dismissing the kid frequently, or not being present for them emotionally or physically. Some researchers even suggest that parents who care less are often abusive towards the kids, which is a form a trauma the kid may never recover from. Therefore, it is essential that if neglect or abusive behavior that critically threatens a child's well-being is spotted from any parent your child goes to school with or plays within the neighborhood with, it should be reported immediately. No kid should ever have to grow up in such a situation.

Evidence reveals that parents who were beaten as kids have a high tendency to repeat the same behavior towards their kids with even more intensity (Kim, 2006). The same research also suggests that such parents are also more likely to be uninvolved and distant.

However, if it is circumstantial and not conscious, it is best to improve and be present. During the early ages, kids need someone to look up to. If that authoritative figure remains distant in their lives, it can be extremely hard to build a sound personality.

Examples of Uninvolved Parenting

- You leave a young child unattended in the house while you spend hours shopping or drinking with your friends.
- You don't care how good or poor they are doing at school.
- You don't care if they have bathed or slept on time.

Pros

Although there haven't been many supporters of this style, some do think that uninvolved parenting breeds stronger, self-reliant, and confident children. However, this has nothing to do with parenting as they get stronger because they have no other option. On the whole, this style of parenting is one of the least preferred parenting styles, and not many kids raised this way become a successful, well-rounded adult.

Cons

Adding more to the list, some other prominent features and behaviors depicted by the children raised by neglecting parents include a confused state of mind, inability to regulate emotions, difficulty in forming fulfilling relationships, and they are mostly anxious and antisocial. They also deal with depression in the later stages of life unless they find a way to overcome childhood distress.

Authoritarian Parenting

As the name suggests, parents who follow an authoritarian approach are the strictest parents of all. They set extremely high standards for their children, believe in rewards and punishment, and rarely show any affection towards their kids. It isn't like they don't love their kids. They just don't believe in expressing affection openly. They think it is what weakens the children. They don't let any misbehavior take place, and in case it does, there is punishment involved. There is little communication, and the child is expected to follow a number of rules and regulations without actually knowing why. Kids who are raised in this manner are usually obedient in general, but that obedience is a result of fear. They don't engage in things because they enjoy doing them, but because they are fearful that if they are not completed, there might be grave consequences.

Examples of Authoritarian Parenting

Authoritarian parents think that it is either their way or the highway. An example of this can be your child is prohibited from dating anyone or engage in any interaction with the opposite gender.

They may also be forbidden from going over for night stays, have to fall asleep at sharp 9:00 p.m. every night, or not watch TV for more than 2 hours per day.

You can clearly note that these instructions have a consequence associated with them. The parent is trying to instill fear in the child and also trying to bribe them to do better.

Pros

People who support this theory believe that this form of parenting does raise well-behaved and well-mannered individuals. They have their expectations set high and are dedicated. They are careful about indulgence and are better at resisting temptations. They also have their priorities set straight, have goals they want to achieve, and also know of the steps required to turn them into reality.

Cons

The opposition of this parenting style agrees that the kids raised under authoritarian parenting are obedient, but they also rank low on self-esteem and happiness. They think they are never good enough for anyone or anything, and this lack of confidence causes unhappiness. Since they have been told all their childhood to stay focused on their goals and careers, they also face difficulty in forming social relationships and prefer independence.

Free-Range Parenting

Free-range parenting was something that became a debatable topic when a mother, Lenore Skenazy, was criticized for letting her nine-year-old boy take the subway all alone. Everyone critiqued the mother for not having any consciousness or heart. She was publicized throughout New York as a symbol of bad parenting. Her response to all that criticism came in published form in 2009 in her book, where she not only gave solid explanations for her behavior but also gave rise to the term free-range parenting. After its publication, some researchers got on board to support her ideology about parenting, and later many parents associated themselves with being one.

Despite the bad press it received, free-range parenting isn't careless parenting. It is just a style that doesn't involve micromanaging every activity of the child. According to Lenore, it is wrong to think that parental supervision is required 24/7. The kids are not in any danger and can be left to enjoy some carefree time on their own to explore.

If we come to think of it, the idea is pretty simple. It is about letting your child have some unsupervised time and let the parents have some me-time. Of course, frequent visits to the room they are in is a compulsion, but the kids can still be left to engage in free play, experiment with things on their own, build self-confidence and explore their surroundings without being judged, questioned, or instructed.

Examples of Free-Range Parenting

- You watch from a distance while your kid plays in the park.
- You let them walk on an empty street without holding their hands. However, you are always just a step behind.
- You let your child plenty of unscheduled activities, such as playing a pick-up game with their neighbors

or playing with their dog in the backyard with minimal supervision.

- You allow kids to earn independence and focus on teaching them to try new things on their own.

Pros

Free-range parenting helps kids be more creative and innovative. They are self-reliant, thus, less likely to get bullied by others. They have a greater sense of self-esteem as they aren't questioned about their decisions, and they are more independent in general as they have been taking care of things themselves for a long time. They also have no difficulty building new relationships and usually have larger social circles. Finally, they are also great with the regulation of their emotions and are less likely to grow up to be dependent on others.

Cons

The only downfall of this parenting style is the treatment parents receive. They are called irresponsible, labeled bad, and considered a danger to their kids as there are many ideas on the level of freedom kids should be allowed to have. Moreover, parents may also face some legal ramifications based on the state or country they live in.

Permissive Parenting

Remember we talked about authoritarian parenting earlier? Now imagine something exactly the opposite of that. No stringent rules and regulations, no punishments, or the fear of consequences; this is what permissive parenting is all about. It is indulging in the whims of your kid. It is about avoiding all forms of punishment, consequences or confrontations. The goal of this parenting style is to build a stronger bond between the parent and the child with the intention of becoming their friend. Permissive parents, according to experts, don't set unachievable expectations for their kids, are lenient, and rarely discipline their kids as they believe in free will and age-appropriate behaviors. They give in to their children's urges without thinking and just want the best for them.

Examples of Permissive Parenting

Not stopping your kids from trying new things as they have complete freedom to make decisions for themselves. When the kids make mistakes, the parents don't punish. They just talk about them as they think that kids stick to behaviors they think are good and avoid the bad ones. An example of this can be your kids sleeping later than usual a few nights just because they want to, or wishing to skip school. As a parent, you don't push them into going but rather hope that they will eventually learn of the consequences of missing school in the form of extra work and poor grades.

However, this style of parenting doesn't necessarily mean that the parents are irresponsible. They do keep their eyes open and don't intentionally set their children up for failure.

Pros

The biggest perk of this style of parenting is that a strong bond between the child and the parent is created built on trust. The child knows that they are trusted with their decisions and the parent knows that even when the child makes a mistake, they will know how to handle it themselves. The kids are more open-minded, independent, and confident.

Cons

Children brought up in such households have trouble with authority and therefore don't do well in academia or professional careers, as they are not used to having someone dictate things to them. This also makes it harder for them to regulate the many emotions they feel. This confusion can result in unhappiness, too.

Does Parenting Style Influence Success?

There is little research with concrete evidence to determine that a certain parenting style has a significant influence on the future success of a child. Each household is different. Even if two households are run on the same parenting style, one can't be certain that the children raised will be identical as the parenting style alone is not enough to account for children's behavior. There are several other external factors at play here. Even if we talk about the upbringing of kids in the same household, not every child will develop the same personality and ambition in life.

In an ideal situation, researchers might conduct some controlled experiments where the chances of any external factors influencing the upbringing will be eliminated. However, one still can't say it will be a 100% guarantee that both kids will have the same intellectual capacity or will be as successful as the other. Since there is little hope that this will work, researchers have nothing but to rely on the present evidence in front of them. So far, research to this date has offered the following insights:

- Children raised under the authoritative parenting style appears to be more well-behaved and successful. They tend to be more resourceful, socially-adept, and emotionally-sound. They also do well in school and professional life.

- Most kids raised in uninvolved households are the least developed among their peers. According to one study, most of the juvenile offenders come from neglected families (Steinberg, 2001).

- Kids raised under the authoritarian parenting style usually depict aggressiveness and defiant behaviors. They report having depression, poor self-esteem, and suffer from stress and anxiety more often.

- Kids raised under the permissive parenting style are less likely to depict any aggression or unmanageable behavioral problems. They are also emotionally intelligent, empathetic, and creative. However, that doesn't mean that they do well in school because research suggests otherwise.

Why Parenting Sometimes Goes Wrong

As discussed earlier, there is no proven formula to identify which parenting style works best for kids. While talking about the outcomes of each, there are some things that many parents (regardless of the parenting style they follow) do that affect the child negatively. Therefore, it is best that we identify these practices to limit some of the misbehavior and disobedience. With scientific research backing each claim, researchers view them as the primary blunders parents make, which leads to mental health problems, anxiety, stress, and depression in the life of the child as they mature. They call them the mistakes that result in the "unsuccessfulness" of kids.

They Use Harsh Punishments

Spanking, in particular, is one of those things that can become traumatic for kids when exposed to it during early childhood. Parents who use spanking as a means to straighten out their kids and teach them some discipline do more damage than good, as research shows that spanking leads to hyperactivity, oppositional behavior, and aggression (Ferguson, 2013). This means that after some time, the kid stops fearing it and repeats the behavior again. It is because they already know what's coming, and since they have had a taste of it in the past, it no longer has an impact on them as before. Research based on studies conducted on 160,000 children over a 50-year span revealed that kids who are beaten in their childhood are more likely to develop mental health problems as they mature and suffer from cognitive difficulties too (Gershoff & Grogan-Kaylor, 2016).

They Yell A Lot

Research suggests that verbal discipline using harsh words and commands that involve shouting, insults, or cursing is detrimental in the upbringing of the children and not a healthy behavior to exhibit in the presence of them (Wang & Kenny,

2014). Such yelling and insulting have many negative repercussions, such as depressive symptoms, poor academic performance, lack of self-confidence, and other behavioral issues. It also increases the likelihood of them growing up to become as verbally abusive as their parents when in relationships. Since they view it as a normalized behavior, they are more likely to adopt it.

They Make the Kids Dependent

Independence is an essential skill to develop in kids from an early age. Some experts suggest training them to sleep from as early as six months. Sleep training allows them to go back to sleep on their own upon waking up in the middle of the night. This shows how important it is to teach them to be independent and autonomous. Evidence reveals that parents who psychologically control their kids results in negative outcomes for their kids. Children raised under these parents report less confidence and self-worth (Garber, Robinson, & Valentiner, 1997).

Encouraging kids to be independent at an early age helps them with conflict resolution and to create meaningful interpersonal relationships. It is easy to assume that kids who are self-reliant are more confident in nature and approach new things with passion without any fear of failure.

They Allow Them to Watch TV from an Early Age

Some ten years ago, no one would have thought about placing the baby in front of the screen and leaving them to take in all that is happening on the television. However, in a world where our phones and tablets have become our new TV sets, it is very common to find one in the hands of an infant. Parents have always relied on some good TV time for the kids so that they can catch a breath of their own, but research suggests it is concerning. In 2007, one study proposed that parents who allow their kids to watch TV before the age of three hinder their participation and vocabulary and increases their chances of growing up to be a bully in school (Zimmerman, Christakis, & Meltzoff, 2007). TV usage for longer periods of time causes attention problems and can lead to impaired math and learning proficiency.

Their Cell Phone Usage Around Kids is High

Parents who don't attend to their children's needs with 100% commitment or remain distracted by their phones around kids cause a delay in their child's development. The kid feels less valued and unimportant and grows up to be shy and less confident. Our technology-induced attention has also given rise to emergency room visits in recent years, as suggested by one article (Worthen, 2012).

Can We Change the Way We Parent?

Yes! And no. The answer isn't clear, as we can't be certain about the degree of change required. It isn't something you can change overnight since most of the behaviors we exhibit weren't learned in a day. One can't wake up feeling different one day after reading a book or watching an inspirational movie. Parenting isn't just a collection of some basic rules or skills. It is influenced by a number of things such as the culture and traditions your family follows, the sort of personality you and your spouse have, and the kind of kid you are dealing with.

Moreover, since there is not much research to determine what parenting style is the best as researchers rarely follow up with parenting, it is hard to tell what suits your customized needs. However, some studies suggest that kids who grow up under authoritative-style parenting show higher chances of success in life and seem more disciplined and well-mannered. They also have better grades in school and more confidence overall. Their emotional stability is also sounder than other parenting styles, raising their chances to succeed.

Lastly, keep in mind that there is no perfect formula for parenting. Even authoritative parenting doesn't guarantee well-behaved children as it isn't the only factor that shapes their personalities. Therefore, the best you can do is read through the pros and cons mentioned above and adopt different practices if you think you need a change in your parenting style.

If you are interested in taking a Parenting Style quiz, we recommend a short 2-minute quiz from PsychCentral. Here's the link to the quiz:

https://psychcentral.com/quizzes/parenting-style-quiz/

Chapter 4: Misbehavior – It's Always Going to Happen (And What to Do About It)

Although it's an old saying that kids will be kids, we have been noticing the increasing aggressiveness and anger in them. They seem to be more violent, short-tempered, and, most of all, undisciplined. They exhibit such behaviors not just at their homes in front of their parents but also in public places, schools, and many other places they are at. And the worst part is, you can never see it coming. Of course, there are some visible signs such as a bad mood in the morning or an urge to say no to everything, but their actions, in recent times, have been more expressive and that is concerning.

As parenting experts, we deal with clients every day complaining about misbehavior. We talk about the many causes and factors and try and come up with a practical plan of action to limit it to an extent. But what we really need is to identify the root causes of why kids are acting out so much these days.

Firstly, they are not sick. Every day, we come across a new disorder that makes normalized behavior look suspicious. Every kid is different. Just because one is calm and composed and the other one running places doesn't mean there is something wrong with the second one. That too, for a toddler or teenager, is acceptable behavior. Therefore, the first thing we want to tell you is to stop looking at them as if something is wrong with them. No need to browse symptoms that are considered normal otherwise and label the child "in need of help".

The second important thing to note here is that one of the most common reasons children misbehave is because they aren't getting the type of attention they used to before. Ask yourself, was your mother busy watching TV all day and feeding you processed meat? Was she always against you going out and playing? Do you see the problem here? A lack of attention.

Kids feel invisible because parents have their eyes dug into phones and laptops while making frozen mac n' cheese.

Although these don't encompass everyone, one key factor which many researchers believe is what causes misbehavior, is the lack of discipline. But disciplining isn't always positive. In most cases, as parents, we resort to the negative kind and use fear, consequences, and punishments for keeping them out of something. Some of us put fear into our kids' heads by telling them that if they don't behave well, they will get a sound beating. We tell them that there will be consequences for the way they act. We scare them with things like "no Wi-Fi", "no TV", "no going out", etc. Positive disciplining doesn't involve any of that but rather a set of certain rules and regulations where communication and understanding are the foundation. There is trust, empathy, and of course, disciplining but in a way that doesn't seem enforced. But before we discuss that in detail and how to get started with the approach, it is essential that we comprehend why kids act the way they do and what factors play a key role in shaping their behavior.

Are Parents Encouraging Their Kids to Misbehave?

Remember the time when we were little kids, and one death stare from our parents over something wrong we did or said would freeze every last cell into our bodies? How cold was that stare? We would silently pray that our parents would forget all about it in the car because we knew the minute we walked into the house, all hell would break loose. All for because we dropped a few crumbs of cake on our shirt? Because we unintentionally pushed someone while we were playing hide and seek? Some of us surely will remember and agree, right? It wasn't that we were obedient kids or born well-mannered. It was the influence and authority our parents had on us that shaped our entire system.

So tell us that you don't wonder why kids today don't act as obedient? Why are they determined to do the opposite of what you ask of them? Are they trying to get back at you for something? If not, then maybe your parenting is at fault. In his book, Dr. Kevin Leman asks some similar questions from parents.

Why does it feel that the kids are deliberately disobeying us? Why do they diss their parents? Why do they seem so disrespectful? Why the hitting, pulling, and cussing? Why do parents have to use threatening and cajoling to get somewhere with them? Why do they have to pull out all their guns so that their kids will show some respect? Most important: what has gotten into kids. Why are they acting like zombies?

It is time we acknowledge that parenting has changed from the time the TV was monochromatic. One of the biggest challenges parents faced is the influence of technology on our children. Certain content on the TV and internet has instilled the wrong message into our children's minds. Misbehavior is depicted as a comedy on TV shows, cartoons, and movies. When kids see that, they replicate the same behaviors. Substance abuse, poor family structure, and defiant toward authority figures are widely shown on TV. There is so much more we can go on about because clearly as parents, we are as frustrated too. We want them to have good values, yet there is only so much control we have on what our kids are exposed to on the internet. How are we expecting our kids to behave and respect others when they are exposed to hours of misbehavior depicted on TV and social media?

Even though we may have put parental control on the TV and computer, still this doesn't completely eradicate potential adverse influence. So what can be done, really?

According to Leman, one major reason why kids behave the way they do is that parents are encouraging them to. Shocking, right? We, adults, aren't stopping them, which is why they have become the way they are. Leman thinks that our family structures and who gets to have the last say matters the most. He says that as parents, we are so concerned about hurting our children's feelings that we give in to all of their demands and requests, even when they are out of proportion so that the child is happy. That, to him, is bad parenting.

At the end of the day, no one wants to play the good cop, bad cop. We all want to be friends with our children instead of their mentors. In doing so, we let them roll over us and take charge. Suddenly, they become the ones who get to have the last say in the house. But Leman also argues that isn't it like deliberately set up for failure? Think about it, they may have an edge over us in the house, but they will struggle when in the academic or professional life. There, when they see others in charge and made to follow a set of rules and regulations, the adjustment will become harder for them. So, in a way, the structure you set in your house will eventually cause their demise.

Another way parents set up their children for misbehavior is by not having a parenting game plan. What does a parenting game plan look like, you may ask? Imagine you have been asked to coach a team of professional footballers. You are the one who decides who gets to play at what position, what strategies of passing the ball shall be implemented, and what will be the level of training each player requires. Now, imagine you don't have a plan. You don't do any training. You don't invest your time teaching them how to play, how to pass the ball, and how to defend. What are your chances of winning a game against anyone? How do you think your team will perform without any guidelines or knowing what everyone has to do?

The same applies to parenting. Not having a course of action is equivalent to their defeat. They don't even stand a chance at attempting to win unless by some miracle. No parent wants that for their children, which is why some ground rules have to be implemented from day one. Make it your goal to instill in them good morals and values so that they are ready to tackle anything once they grow up. It is your job to train them, motivate them, work on them, and build their confidence. They need to understand what behaviors are acceptable and which aren't. They need to know what actions will result in rewards and what actions will have consequences.

The second biggest mistake that parents make is exercising a lack of consistency. Kids have relentless minds. Once an idea gets stuck, it has to happen. They are quick to latch onto promises made by their parents and will remember them for days, weeks, or even years. So promising them a new soccer ball at the end of the exams and not living up to that promise makes it harder for them to respect you. Therefore, aim for consistency and only promise them things you can offer. Inconsistency gives them a reason to control their parents. Therefore, you must show them, at all times, who is in charge of things. Once they acknowledge that, they will respect you and stay disciplined.

What Influences Child Behavior?

Do you recall the time when your kid was considered the most well-mannered and disciplined child on the block? It wasn't long before they turned into their little terror selves and gave you a hard time with nearly everything. They are nagging about their food choices, resisting sleep, misbehaving with you, throwing things at their siblings, crying and whining, making excuses, fighting about control, and hurting the feelings of everyone around them. Looks like their personality took a 360-degree turn, doesn't it? However, this shift doesn't happen overnight. It takes some time at first and then suddenly engulfs you whole.

This transition from the purest little soul to an out-of-control demon makes you feel frustrated and helpless. No wonder you feel like failing at parenting. But you aren't the only one. We deal with so many clients discussing the same worries and concerns they have when dealing with an out of control child.

We tell them that some kids are easier to deal with. They are easy to parent. But there are rarely any fool-proof strategies that work like magic for everyone. Just because something worked for your sister's daughter doesn't mean it will work for you too.

Fatigue

Sleep deprivation or fatigue can make even the most angelic of us turn into monsters. We function poorly, our energy levels are low, everything irritates us or ruins our mood, our mind seems foggy, we can't think clearly, and we have a difficult time dealing with others around us.

All these are the negative effects of fatigue and sleep deprivation. If they can have such a powerful effect on adults, imagine what it does to our little ones.

Their level of fatigue determines how good or bad they will be in terms of their behavior and mood. If they seem stressed, anxious, or fatigued, you can expect tantrums and whining.

Low Expectations

Kids are always trying to please us. However, they want to know what will please you. They need some expectations to live up to. If you keep labeling them with how difficult they are, they will act out your expectations. Conversely, if you tell them how good, well-mannered and disciplined they are, they will try to live up to that. The right labels have the power to alter a child's behavior. At the same time, setting achievable expectations of them also makes them accountable for their actions. Having no expectations or viewing them as a lost cause will undermine their personality, and they will be on your nerves all the time to prove their worthiness.

No Say in Important Decisions

No matter how small they are age-wise, kids love to be treated like adults. They want their own cutlery on the dinner table, want to tie their own laces, comb hair themselves, and have the remote to themselves.

However, when they are treated as kids, that doesn't sit well with them. Research suggests that when kids are included in the process of decision-making, it allows them to think, act, and behave like an adult. They feel valued and heard and, thus, throw fewer tantrums or cause unrest. Therefore, parents should allow their children to be an active decider of the things in their lives within a controlled process. Instead of enforcing rules on them, how about asking them if they feel like doing it now or later? For example, instead of telling them to get into the bath, you could try asking them if they would like to take a bath now or an hour later. On the one hand, you are reminding them that a bath is due and on the other, you are giving them the control to decide when they want to take it.

A Lack of Routines

A lack of routine poses a negative impact on a kid's behavior. They thrive on schedules. According to Kim John Payne, author of *Simplicity Parenting*, set routines lead to calmer, more secure, and happier kids. When kids know what to expect next, they prepare themselves prior to the activity. For instance, scheduling a nap time right after you bathe them prepares them mentally for it before they even sit in the tub. Schedules also make parenting easier as parents are left with some free time on their hands at the end of their day, thanks to the routines they have in practice. The same can be applied to other areas such as what food they will have on a particular day, what activities they can enjoy over the weekend, what places they will visit on a free day, etc., etc. Therefore, aim for predictability.

There can be a number of different things that affect a child's behavior. Sometimes, they behave a certain way only to seek your attention. Other times, there is something graver affecting them or making them lose their sanity. Therefore, it is important that we highlight those influences first before moving on to learn what actually makes them misbehave.

Nutrition

Nutrition serves as a changing instrument in the way a child behaves. It wasn't known until recent studies proved how crucial the right diet can be in the way kids act and behave. Although more work needs to be done, we now have some evidential data that gluten-free diets help children to be less difficult. Some other studies also suggest that banning certain types of high-energy inducing foods from their diets can reduce their hyperactivity and anxiety (Pelini, 2018). For instance, some kids become agitated when they have high sugar content in their bodies. They become more aggressive, and bedtime becomes difficult. Asking them to sit in one place is a hurdle on its own. And besides, for centuries, we have been preached by the monks that we are what we eat. If we fill our bodies with fatty and greasy foods, we are bound to feel fatigued and lethargic, and we have all been a witness to the severe results of a missed nap, haven't we?

Foods have also been linked with our mood alterations. Ever had that feeling where you just wanted to gulp down a pint of Ben & Jerry's? Your kids are no different. Therefore, the best way to stabilize their mood and improve their chances of staying disciplined is to start by feeding them the right foods.

Sometimes, kids find it difficult to react to emotions. They lack emotional understanding. They have only been familiarized with certain emotions such as anger, anxiety, or fear. However, when they come across sadness, loss, or frustrations, they don't know what to make of them. So they do the things they know of like lashing out or staying quiet in the case of fear. Staying quiet out of fear is one of the most common reasons for sexual assaults among young children. Despite knowing their predator's name, they take years before coming forward. Sometimes, they simply begin to misbehave. Their way of manifesting different emotions can come out in multiple ways too. If they had a bad dream last night, they might seem reluctant to go to sleep or want you to sleep with them. If you deny that, they might lash out or begin to cry.

Why Do Kids Act Out and Misbehave?

Every parent has dealt with misbehavior at some point. Sometimes, it is just a phase that passes quickly, and sometimes, it keeps recurring from time to time. However, as parents, we must understand that kids are like sponges. They will eventually take in all that they see around themselves. We have had parents come to us complaining about how their middle son would keep hitting the younger sister with whatever he had in his hands. What they failed to self-analyze was that he was being exposed to violence from video games that his eldest brother played all day. That behavior became so normalized in his state of mind that he started enacting it in real life. Remember the time we would try moves from WWE on our younger siblings too? The point is, kids will misbehave if they are being exposed to it from a source.

But that isn't the only reason. Sometimes, there can be some underlying issues that need addressing first. Misbehavior can often be a reaction rather than an action. They act out because something bothers them. So what could be those reasons?

Let's figure it out together below.

They Are Testing If Rules Will Be Enforced

Children are always trying to figure out new stuff. They are curious about their boundaries and which actions will be rewarded and what actions will be punished. To pique their curiosity, they keep testing their primary caregivers: the parents. They want to know what boundaries exist. Therefore, they sometimes misbehave and, other times, act well-mannered.

They Want To Assert Themselves As Independent

By the time a child turns two, their journey to self-discovery begins. As they are learning to walk and talk, they want to gain more control over the things that concern them. They want to have a say in what they will eat, when they will sleep, what they will wear, and so on and so on. In the process of gaining autonomy and control, they may use misbehavior as a method to exert their independence from their parents and form their identity.

Their Basic Needs Aren't Meant

We already talked about nutrition and fatigue and their effect on a child's mood and behavior. If any of their basic needs aren't met, they are going to act out. They will cry more, misbehave more, and might even throw in a tantrum or two. Although this is only a temporary state, it is best to avoid keeping them waiting.

They Lack Experience

When kids try something for the first time, they don't know if there are any rules they should follow. For instance, if you and your child are on the road and all of a sudden, they let go of your hand and cross the street without looking both ways, it is only because they don't know that's what they are supposed to do first. Since it is something unexpected for the caregiver too, chances are they will lash out at the child for the sake of their own safety. However, the lashing won't be greeted with a smile, for sure. So sometimes, misbehavior is the result of a lack of knowledge and experience.

They Mimic Our Actions

If our children see us, parents, treat others (our own parents, our spouses, our friends, etc.) a certain way, they will soon pick up similar behavior. There have been cases where an abusive parent blames his/her/their own parent for normalizing abuse in the house. Your home is the first teaching institution your children enroll in. If they see you screaming and yelling and shouting, they will scream, yell, and shout too. If you have the habit of enforcing punishments harshly, they will use similar harshness to express their anger. If they have been hearing insults and cuss words, they are going to add them to their little vocabulary too.

If this sort of behavior is prevalent in the house, it isn't hard to assume that the kid will likely grow up repeating the behavior unless parents make a conscious effort to break the toxic cycle.

Positive Discipline – What Is It?

As briefly discussed earlier, positive parenting is a way of guiding and teaching kids about certain behaviors that are acceptable and also the ones that aren't. It is about laying guidelines and providing them with step by step roadmap to get there. It doesn't merely involve enforcing rules but rather is a subtle but firm way of getting things done. Positive discipline, unlike punishments, revolves around eliminating undesirable behaviors using positive and uplifting means. The idea is to foster the relationship between the parent and the child so that both can openly communicate the expectations of each other. Parents can let the kids know what is expected of them and also take a step further to tell them what behaviors will help them fulfill those expectations.

It was first suggested by Jane Nelson, the author of the parenting bestseller *Positive Discipline: The Classic Guide to Helping Children Develop Self-Discipline, Responsibility, Cooperation, and Problem-Solving Skills*. According to Jane, even a casual and mundane moment can turn into a full-on power struggle with a child. Therefore, instead of yelling, shouting and issuing punishments, this method allows kids to understand what is expected of them in that particular moment without the parent having to increase the pitch of their voice or give them the angry eyes. It is common knowledge that humans, no matter how young or old they are, learn best in a connected and safe environment. This is what parents try to achieve through positive disciplining. If you just remember this one very important thing, you will be off to a good start here:

COMMUNICATION comes before CORRECTION.

Importance of Positive Discipline

- It teaches kids self-discipline, responsibility, cooperation, and problem-solving.
- It strengthens relationships and builds trust.
- It makes both the parent and child respect each other.
- It improves a child's self-esteem and confidence.
- It allows children to contribute in various ways and feel significant.
- It helps children manage their emotions and deal with stress in a healthy manner.

Getting Started with Positive Parenting

Now that we are aware of its significance and how crucial it can be to help parents deal with misbehavior in a non-violent way, here are practical ways to get started with enforcing positive discipline in kids.

Treat the Disease

Every action is a reaction to something. Your goal is to find that cause and treat it. For instance, if your child has started using cuss words, the reaction shouldn't be to punish them, but first, recognize where they are learning them from. The first step will be limiting their exposure to the place or environment and then move on to disciplining them. Once we understand the root cause, we will minimize their chances to act that way.

Give Them Attention

Kids often act out because they feel ignored. They will do anything to seek attention from you, even if it means misbehaving. A child that constantly vies for their parent's attention reveals the unhealthiness of the relationship. See if they are trying to tell you something repeatedly using misbehavior or if they are just attention-deficient. Whichever is the case, positively disciplining them using open communication can prove effective.

As a parent myself, I understand how demanding parent duties can be. After staying up all night to take care of a sick child, working 8-10 hours a day, or completing all the house chores, it can be very difficult to summon the energy to give your child the quality playtime and attention they need. For some of us, building a fort, playing hide and seek, or doing other physical activities with our kids is not something we desire to do during our downtime. If you find yourself in this boat, my suggestion is to find an activity that you find relaxing and enjoyable and let your kid join in. For example, let them join you for your morning walk or listen to an audiobook with them. Other activity ideas that require less physical activity from parents can be hosting a dance party, and you be the judge. You can also let your child do a pretend play with stuffed animals or create a scavenger hunt game for them. For the scavenger hunt, it requires a bit of creativity. You have to come up with different things for your children to find. For example, tell your children to go take a picture of something that is smaller than their hands. All you have to do is give them the list of things they need to find, and meanwhile, you can kick back and rest on the couch.

Offer Productive Means to Contribute

As stated earlier, kids count on your attention. They want to feel valued, and one of the best ways to make them feel so is by asking for them to contribute. Tell them that you need their help with things. That is the best way to counter an attention-deficient child as not only do they feel valued, but they also feel important. Tell them that you need help with cleaning the kitchen, tidying up the room, or shopping for groceries. What you are essentially doing is allowing them to seek your attention in productive ways that don't involve crying and whining.

Aim to Lead, Not Control

The moment they realize that someone is trying to tame them into being good, they will retaliate. Take the example of any great world leader. Did they rule with control or leadership? Instead of shouting orders at them to go brush their teeth before bedtime, ask them if they want their teeth to look squeaky clean or yellowish? Or use the consequences tactic, which allows the kids to know what will happen if they don't do what they've been asked to do. In this example, you can tell them that when people don't brush their teeth every night, their teeth start to fall out after some days. What you are doing is preventing resistance without using force. You are leading them towards goal completion by pushing them from behind using positive reinforcement. More importantly, you aren't telling them blandly what they should do. You are giving them the control and hoping that they will make a sane decision. When they know that they aren't being manipulated into doing something forcefully, they don't resist. Instead, they respect you for giving them a chance to decide for themselves.

Be the leader, not the controller. Threatening them might lead to some temporary success, but it won't work in the long run. So don't set yourself up for disappointment. Children behave and cooperate when they see us as their allies instead of adults policing them.

Avoid Time-outs

Time-outs seem like the easiest alternative parents use to give themselves some peace of mind. However, when it is overused, it may do the opposite, and the child might act out more to gain your attention. So what is a viable solution? How about a "time-in" instead of a time out? Instead of telling them to go into their rooms, how about sitting with them and talking about the issue at hand? Let them sort things out and talk about what bothered them. Then, make them see where they were wrong, and once they are ready, tell them that they should apologize. If all goes as planned, they will avoid throwing a tantrum and prefer expressing over all the yelling and shouting.

Hear Them Out

Being heard and getting attention may seem synonymous, but they aren't. Being heard means hearing out their ideas, complaints, and requests rather than just attending to their basic needs. Show them that they have a voice, and you are all set to listen. Better yet, as the kids start school, set up a time each day to sit with them and inquire about their day. Ask them to tell you about all the things that happened at school today. Ask them if they have any friends or if they like their teacher. You can even ask if there is something they would like to change about you. They may not have the right words, but they surely will tell you what they would like to change. For example, they might not like how you treat them at the dinner table by cutting their bread into small chunks. They might want to do it themselves. Let them present their case and resolve any grievances they might hold. This will help you two get on the same page and avoid any future conflicts and acting out. Make sure your tone of voice is fun and loving. Using the wrong tone of voice when asking your children questions can make the conversation feel more like an unwanted interrogation than a bonding time.

Use Redirection to Engage Them Elsewhere

One of the greatest things about kids is that they have a short attention span. Apparently, every other thing is as excited as the first one, which means it isn't hard to engage them elsewhere when they are difficult to handle. If you find them walking towards the stairs area, call them into the room to play with something else. If they have picked up any sharp object like a knife, fork, or scissors, give them something else to play with without forcefully grabbing it away from their tiny hands. The idea is to stop them from doing the current activity and be engaged in another one without being told no. When we tell kids too often what they can't do or shouldn't do, they feel irritated. They don't want to be coached about their choices. So they act out in retaliation. So, always say no in a way that doesn't involve the word. When you keep the tone positive and cheerful, it reduces the chances of misbehavior and arguments.

Praise Good Behavior

Don't ever let good behavior go unappreciated. When they feel that their good behavior isn't celebrated by their parents, they are less likely to repeat it. Don't let them think that their good actions go unnoticed or else they will stop doing them altogether. As parents, we always fall short on the compliments part. We are first to point out their wrongdoings but aren't too supportive or acknowledging of the good things they do. We just think that it is what they should be doing in the first place, so what's the point of appreciating? However, when we give negative things more attention instead of positive ones, we are indirectly telling kids that bad behavior is a way to get our attention. So they misbehave more and do less reward-worthy things.

Show Them They Are Priority

It is often hard to allot a dedicated time to attend to your kids, but its importance can't be stressed enough. Making them a priority by giving them the gift of your time makes them feel like they belong and are significant. This also serves as a means to strengthen the bond between the parent and the child, and the goal is to establish some ground rules to prevent misbehavior using positive discipline. When you two share a strong and deeper bond, the chances of them acting out or misbehaving with you decreases. If anything, they will be eager to please you in any way they can as they will begin viewing you as their friend instead of their parent.

To begin, separate half an hour or an hour solely for them. Use that time to bond with them. Read them a story, help them with their homework, and engage in some fun-filled activities like coloring or differentiating between different colors or remembering the names of all the animals they can think of. A loved and happy child is less likely to cause chaos in the house or misbehave with others.

Be Empathetic

Parenting shouldn't be stressful and chaotic, it should be rewarding and fun, says Jim Fay, the creator of the Love and Logic website. He suggests that rather than treating defiant behavior with anger and a long, irritated lecture, how about dealing with it with empathy? There is no need for two people to be angry at the same time. Be the older one and act responsibly. If a child does something out of anger, don't repeat the same and normalize that reaction. Instead, treat the incident with empathy. For instance, if your child starts throwing his toys because you just told them that playtime was over, instead of yelling and directing them to not throw or else there will be consequences, tell them that behavior is upsetting you. Tell them that you wish they would stop doing that as it is making you uncomfortable. Letting them know that their actions are hurting someone and hoping that they will take the hint and stop is a strategic way of dealing with it.

But this works only for younger kids. For older kids, you have to add an element of consequence for some time in the future. Tell him/her that if they don't stop doing it, they will be responsible for their actions. Once they calm down a little, go to them and try to converse with them by talking about their actions. Let them absorb the extent of the damage they could have done and let them take that in. For example, if a teenager was throwing away his video game CDs out of anger, remind them that if they hadn't stopped then, they would have broken them and squandered the chance to play them ever again.

Don't Let Them Argue

A lot of times, parents think that arguing allows the child to speak their minds and let their angst and frustration out. True, but arguments also tumble the authoritative structure of the parents in the house. As your child enters grade school, they are developing their self-identity and learning to be more independent. They also have a better grasp of language skills, and sometimes they are determined to get the last word in every discourse. So how should you handle when your child wants to have the last word? Or should you even let your child have the last word? There is no easy answer to this. To be honest, I am working on this dilemma, as well. I cannot tell you what will work best in your family, but here's what I found that seems to work for my children and me. The key to handling a discourse is the parent's attitude. It is useless for us as a parent to feel defensive or intimidated by a child's verbal aggravation. Sometimes the best reply to a child's last word is to ignore it. However, other times when they cross the line, it is important for you to address it. You can acknowledge your child's feelings by saying, "Honey, I know you are angry" or limit their actions by telling them, "I will not allow you to throw things when you are angry." Then let your child know what you will tolerate and what the consequences are if they cross the line. Make sure the consequences are reasonable and that you follow through with what you say. The limit of tolerance varies from parents to parents. Personally, I don't mind my children having the last word if, in the end, they do what I ask them to do, if their words do not involve profanity, or if their words are not a personal remark about my character and values. I suggest parents think through the possible discourse scenarios before they happen. This will help you be less reactive and more proactive when the situation occurs.

Don't Let Them Feel Ashamed of Failures

Shame and guilt are two of the most prominent expressions around mistakes and failures. When we immerse ourselves into these negative feelings, these feelings can stop us from trying new things. When we think that failure is a definite outcome, we are less likely to put in the work that's required to succeed. The same happens with kids. Once they make a mistake, they become fearful of giving it another try. They lose their self-confidence and feel like a failure. So the next time we encourage them to give it another try, they reject the idea and misbehave. Encourage them to see their failures as opportunities to learn. Tell them that there is nothing to be ashamed about and share a few of your own failures and mistakes to boost their confidence and remove that fear of failing from their minds.

Chapter 5: Why Emotional Intelligence Is So Important

Raising kids who are emotionally-intelligent and conscious is every parent's goal. However, it is also something that doesn't receive as much limelight as it should, considering it is one of those things that helps parents raise kids with a fulfilling purpose. This chapter would aim to give emotional intelligence a specific definition and highlight the important role it plays in our lives.

As we have seen, most of the chapters in this book deal with either misbehavior or with instilling good habits in kids. But isn't it strange that most of the advice we have focused on until now deal with the catastrophe after it happens? What if raising kids to become emotionally sound was the key to preventing one in the first place? Shocking, right? It's time we take this leap of faith and prevent our kids from becoming defiant, rebellious, and inconsiderate towards the feelings of others.

We already know what bad behavior is by now. We also know how kids handle it using negative emotions like anger, annoyance, irritation, and angst. The biggest problem here is that we don't teach our kids how to deal with these emotions without causing a scene. We, too, feel cross at times – sometimes at our bosses and spouses or friends – but do we always get into a fight, use cuss words, or start throwing things? No, we rarely show it and act normal. We use other mediums to vent it out. Sometimes, we complain. Other times we just sit down, sip some water (or something stronger), and let the feeling pass on its own. So if we handle the negative experience positively, can we not teach our kids to do the same?

We can, with emotional intelligence.

How an emotion gets treated determines the reaction it will inflict. Some researchers joke about emotional intelligence and call it potty training for our emotions and feelings. But they also emphasize its importance at a young age because this can potentially be the only skill that saves you from spending your child's tuition fee as their bail money.

According to Professor John Gottman, the man who revolutionized parenting, the application of emotional intelligence in parenting wasn't something that he thought of on a bright Sunday morning while taking a shower but something he spent years analyzing.

He called upon 100 married couples with kids aged between 4 and 5. The parents were each handed some questionnaires to fill in. Later, the same parents were called in for several rounds of interviews that lasted for hours at a time. The behaviors, answers, and expressions of the parents were monitored. He even called a number of kids and taped sessions with them while they played with their buddies. The respiration, heart rates, levels of sweat and blood flow were monitored as well. Then, they follow the lives of those kids and families as they grew up throughout adolescence. More rounds of interviews and sessions were conducted at various intervals.

After years of extensive research, Gottman was able to deduce that there are four types of parents. Each category of parents was different from one another based on the way emotions were dealt with within the family. These categories included the following:

Disapproving Parents

According to Gottman, disapproving parents are quite critical of negative emotions. They think that kids who are emotionally-expressive should be punished. They are the ones who think that boys shouldn't cry or that girls shouldn't express anger and should be obedient at all times. The expression of negative emotions is considered a character flaw or weakness. They are quite conservative and judge or criticize harshly.

Dismissing Parents

As the title suggests, such parents ignore, disregard, or belittle negative emotions. They are even worse than the first kind as they don't even acknowledge emotions in the first place. The kids are expected to get over their issues on their own as parents don't think they are worthy of their time and effort. The kids usually grow up thinking of themselves as flawed and lack any emotional stability.

Laissez-Faire Parents

Although this category of parents acknowledges and accepts emotional expression, they offer little guidance on how to handle them. They think of emotional expression as something that just works on its own like a hydraulic press where one simply releases the emotion out of their system and then forgets about it. There are also no limits set on behaviors. Kids brought up by such parents did poorly over time and were trouble-makers battling with self-esteem issues.

Ultra-Parents

Ultra parents or emotional coaches were the best out of the four as they raised emotionally-intellectual children. They were very accepting of their children's emotions, guided them well on how to deal with them, and helped them pave a way to resolve those issues. A child's negative emotions were handled with compassion, respect, and patience and were viewed as an opportunity to enhance intimacy. The kids were more confident, had a great aptitude to develop friendships, and less likely to suffer from self-esteem issues.

What Is Emotional Intelligence?

Emotional intelligence is the ability to control, express, be conscious of, and handle various emotions empathetically and judiciously. It is about knowing how to act in any given situation, how to speak your mind, how to show consideration towards the feelings of others, and how to handle interpersonal relationships. This ability develops differently in everyone. Some kids are emotionally intelligent, while others master the skill while growing up. There is no right age bracket or a tidy linear model to teach kids how to be emotionally sound. It involves learning and mastering the following things:

- Recognizing and perceiving emotions of oneself and others

- Developing emotional consciousness about one's feelings and then those of others

- Identifying the many emotions and how each should be expressed.

- Understanding the role of feelings, facial expressions, tone of voice, body language, and much more in determining our state of mind.

- Labeling behaviors as happy, angry, or sad.

- Naming emotions as they come and go and building an emotional vocabulary for use.

- Comprehending why we feel certain things and not all.

- Bridging the gap between emotion-induced behaviors such as, "I kicked the ball because I was mad".

- Controlling and managing our expressions and not letting them overpower us.

- Knowing which expressions need to be subsided and which need to be reacted on.

- Empathizing with the feelings of others and relating to them on a deeper level.

- Showing sympathy for people, animals or even things.

Telltale Signs of Emotional Intelligence in Children

Kids learn through experience. If they don't like the taste of any fruit or vegetable the first time, they are less likely to give it another try. They also learn through actions. If they see their parents shouting and yelling at each other, they begin to adopt similar behavior without you realizing it. Before you know it, you will be dealing with complaints of how they pulled someone's hair, bit someone, or pushed them. As stated before, they are sponges who absorb whatever they can. They are intuitive naturally, which is why parents have to be extra cautious around them to foster positive habits. Child experts propose that every child goes through a number of milestones in their lives. The first milestone can be pronouncing yes, no, dada, and mama. The second can be attempting to crawl and then walk with assistance and later without the need for it. Then comes years of learning where they begin to learn the language around them, do simple math, differentiate between colors, name animals and things, etc. But there are some that are intrinsic and require little to no parental intervention. For instance, you might have to raise your fingers when teaching them to count, but they might pick up something you dropped without you asking them in the first place. This is them being empathetic and helpful.

Scientists believe some children are born with the tendency to give and help. They will come to console you if they see you cry even when they aren't aware of what they are doing. They will help you stand up when you slip or mimic cleaning with you with whatever piece of cloth they find or just use their bare hands to get rid of the dust. That is empathy. However, it needs some nurturing as anything left untouched can rot away.

So how do you know if your child has emotional intelligence or not? Below are some sure signs that suggest you have gotten lucky with a gentleman or lady! All that is left is to foster that skill and raise them as emotionally intelligent.

They are Unprejudiced

If a kid is open to different opinions, is willing to listen to what others have to say and accept the differences, then they are emotionally intelligent. How so? It is because they are open to ideas coming from others. They don't just want what they want. They listen. They hear. And then they choose. They are open-minded, are willing to understand why someone does something, and what reasons they could have for behaving in that manner before forming an opinion. They are open to exploring all possibilities. This is what makes them compassionate and curious at the same time.

They Cry

Crying is the one thing that comes naturally. It is also the first emotion we are exposed to the minute we are born.

However, as we grow older, we are told to tone it down, suppress it, and act stronger. This suppression of emotion doesn't make one macho but rather emotionally unstable. Crying should be a natural response to tragedy and loss, and children who aren't afraid to express it are the strongest when it comes to regulating their emotions. If you have a kid who becomes emotional watching a cartoon character in need of help, it isn't something to make fun of. It is something to nurture as they are allowing themselves to be expressive and vulnerable. How many of us can say the same about ourselves? When was the last time we vented out all the frustration piling up inside of us? We still think of it as a sign of weakness when, actually, it is the one thing that clears all the fogginess in the brain and helps us think better.

So don't let society or your own parenting stifle your child for crying when they are emotionally touched by something. Tell them that it's alright to cry and let it all out.

They Show Empathy

That is, of course, undebatable. Almost every child who is emotionally intelligent is also empathetic. Kids that are good at regulating their own feelings are also good at recognizing the emotional state of others and offer their compassion as a response. This is something so phenomenal that it boggles scientists to this date. Research shows that kids who are willing to go out of their way to help others in need also happen to be more successful and at peace than others. They also have happier lives and are surrounded by equally lovable souls.

They Like to Converse

They are great at expressing their ideas and putting their thoughts into words. They are always looking for opportunities to have a heart-to-heart with you. They are always inquiring about your day, what you ate, who you met, and so on. They are all about words and love to share things instead of hiding them.

They are Curious

With open-mindedness comes curiosity. They are keen to know anything and everything about everyone. Possibilities intrigue them, ideas tempt them, and new discoveries excite them. It is those kids who keep asking "why" to everything they see, feel, or talk about. They are fascinated by the stories of others, about how they overcome challenges, how they followed their heart and passion, what kept them going, why they chose that path…these are all signs that your little one is emotionally intelligent.

They Are Good Listeners

They are usually the ones their friends rely on for venting out their issues and discussing their problems. They are keen to listen actively and only offer genuine advice when asked. People view them as trustworthy and hold them in high regard.

They Know How to Stay Calm

They are not the ones to lose their calm when things go haywire. It is one of those skills that even adults struggle with at times. However, they are naturally good at regulating their emotions and staying afloat. They understand that no matter how big the problem, there has to be a solution, and instead of being that one guy in the group that dies in the horror movies first after screaming at the top of his lungs, they think, analyze and breathe. They also have a calmer mindset and strategize things rationally. If your kid does that too, he is emotionally competent.

They Know When and How to Pause

Kids speak their minds even if the thing coming out of their mouth makes zero sense. They are unfiltered and pure. When faced with negative emotions, it is expected of them to lose their calm and act out. However, emotionally intelligent kids are better at this. They don't just blurt out the first thought that comes to their mind. Instead, they pause. Then they reflect before responding. They don't just react to things. Instead, they process everything that's going on first, assess it, and then react.

The Role of Parents in Fostering Emotional Intelligence in Kids

Now, if your child didn't exhibit the skills listed earlier, there is still hope, as becoming emotionally intelligent is a trait that can be learned and nurtured. Not every kid exhibits these skills naturally. So let's get down to the basics of how to raise kids who are emotionally intelligent and what role parents have to play in it.

Starting with the very obvious – you need to create a safe space for them to be expressive. They should feel supported, comforted, and accepted. They shouldn't be treated as someone who lacks any experience and thus holds no say. Kids need an outlet to vent to and share the happenings of the day with. Be that!

Next, you have to help them with the labeling of emotions they are going through. They need to know what to expect from a certain feeling and how to not let it overwhelm them. This all starts from when they are able to recognize different emotions as well as be able to distinguish between them. For instance, anger and frustration may feel the same, but they aren't. Frustration usually comes after anger when we realize there is not much that can be done about something. See, this is the difference they need to learn about so that they are able to express their feelings better and learn to cope with them independently. They need to claim ownership of the emotions they feel. Teach them what they should expect with various emotions. For instance, they might want to stomp their feet when angry, smile and laugh when they are happy, have an upside-down smile when they are sad, etc. You can even make it a game by showing them images of people depicting different emotions. Ask them what they think the person is going through so that they can relate better. You can also ask them to pen down their feelings if they are old enough so that they feel less overwhelmed

One technique any parent can use when teaching their children about the various emotions is the Wheel of Emotions (see image attached). This technique is great for navigating emotions and labeling what they are.

Download printable version at:
https://tinyurl.com/download-wheelofemotions or scan the QR code.

Once we are all set on the understanding and labeling of different emotions, the next step involves learning how to overcome them. This is the part where parents need to introduce their kids to healthy means of coping. Teach them the ways to calm down when they are in shock or anxious. This can include many breathing exercises or sitting down and drinking some water. If they are saddened by something, teach them how to cheer themselves up by either distracting themselves elsewhere or crying over it. If they feel stuck, teach them how not to panic and think about getting out of that situation in a healthy way.

Some other helpful activities, such as coloring, journaling, reading jokes, watching a funny video, etc., can also have a calming effect. When your child is in a better state of mind, it will be easier for you and your child to revisit and find ways to resolve the issue that bothers them.

Although we have discussed it several times earlier, there is no harm in emphasizing its importance over and over again. We are living in a time where it has become highly crucial for kids to learn how to empathize. Every day, we interact with many people. We need to be aware of and be able to respect their emotions as well as ours to stay harmonious. Starting now is the approach you need to take, especially if your kid's acting out is always a bit on the dramatic side or you see them being inconsiderate of the feelings of others. Here's what you need to do.

First, validate their emotions. Even if you don't know what they are upset about or crying over, show empathy. For instance, if they keep insisting on going outside and play, and you want them to clean their room first, don't just yell or order. Show them how upset you are that they haven't cleaned their room. Tell them that it is added work that you will have to deal with and how tired that makes you. That is basically telling them that mommy will be too tired to go outside with them because she will have to clean the room but in a more comforting and tactical way.

At the same time, be sure to add statements like "I know how much you want to go to the park. I can see you are disappointed," so they know you aren't purposely delaying the visit outside. It is also empathizing with their feelings.

Be it feelings, overwhelming emotions, or problems, every kid should be taught how to deal with them. Now that we have labeled and empathized with their feelings, the next step involves offering them a solution or guiding them towards it. If the kid is misbehaving because you forgot to get their favorite chips from the grocery store, ask them to come up with at least three ways to resolve the issue instead of crying or being angry about it. That is telling them that you need their input on solving an important issue and also making them independent to think and come up with ideas to deal with their problems. It's like hitting two birds with one stone, right?

The point is, you need to stress building problem-solving skills in them. You have to let them take control of their own problems instead of relying on mommy and daddy to come up with ideas and solutions. Even if their ideas aren't as good and definitive as yours, don't dismiss them. Instead, make them see why they won't work without discouraging them. Pitch in some suggestions so that they can try things differently but not feel completely dependent on you.

Lastly, don't be scared of discussing your own emotions with them. This is probably one of the best ways to foster emotional intelligence. When kids learn that you, too, deal with problems like them but are still able to show up and get the job done every day, they will learn it too. We often make it a point to keep hiding our emotions, especially when we have a young one around the house. We cry in hiding, and we keep ourselves composed even when we feel like punching a wall. Although our aim is to not disturb them, by doing so, we are limiting their exposure to actions they can pick up on. Tell them what is going through your head even when they don't understand most of it. The goal is to make them see that even adults can have problems. They too have feelings and sometimes they also get hurt. But don't just stop there, tell them how you are combating it as well. Give them an insider's guide about how you deal with your emotions. They will eventually pick up on those behaviors. While at it, use the opportunity to tell them how our emotions can sometimes affect the emotions of others, too.

Chapter 6: The Mentor/Friend Dichotomy

We have all envied kids who had cooler parents than us. Their parents were always there cheering them on during football games, making the yummiest of pies for bake day, going out for ice cream sundaes with them, hanging around at home, watching movies with them, and more. The parents were always motivating them, accepting average grades, reassuring them even when they failed…they were our ideals. We wanted them to be our parents. They seemed so cool with everything. It was basically like watching a real-life version of Gilmore Girls in the neighborhood.

Befriending parents has always seemed that way. Millennial parents seem to have taken on the trend recently. They aspire to be their child's best friend. They want to be considered an insightful part in their child's important decisions, snap selfies with them, celebrate birthdays, and enjoy partying with them.

But that is how it looks from a third-person's perspective. Do kids feel the same enthusiasm? Do they consider themselves as lucky? Are the parents okay with this parenting approach?

In this chapter, we are going to be talking about this specifically and look at the pros and cons of befriending kids. We shall also look at the alternative approach to parenting, which focuses on the importance of maintaining some distance from the kids, allowing them to feel independent but, at the same time, be made to follow some rules and regulations.

Since the day a child is born, parents seem to have been making exceptions and sacrifices for their kids. They spent sleepless nights cradling them, countless days changing their nappies, came home early, said no to the carefree lifestyle, and much more. Acting as a cool parent is both exhausting and demanding. On the one hand, they have to manage the household and on the other, give in to the demands of their kids just so that they remain close with them.

If given a choice, every parent would pick being a friend to their kids and not parents. After all, raising kids in today's environment is a big responsibility. Every step has to be taken cautiously and thoughtfully.

But the real question is, can they be both? Can one person be the child's friend and parent both?

If so, shouldn't all parents aim for that amiability and closeness?

Well, the grass isn't greener on the other side. There are some cons to being a child's friend. In fact, research studies show that it can create problems for the parent in the long run as kids don't necessarily see them as authoritative figures, and thus, implementation of rules can become tricky.

But before we get into all that, we need to understand the literal meaning of befriending.

Friendship, in general, means equality for all. It means that both the partners have an equal say in different matters, and opinions of both are appreciated. It is egalitarian in nature. It means no one is in charge or holds any power over the other. However, if we apply the same definition to a parent/child relationship, we instantly start to view how it can be bad. If the parent/child relationship is primarily a friendship, then it puts parents in a difficult situation to have the last say in a matter or implement any restrictions. It means that kids can do whatever they want and not be scolded over their choices. If we come to think of it, doesn't this sound a lot like permissive parenting we discussed in chapter 3 of the book? The kids are a creature of their own. They aren't a part of the herd. They get to make their own rules and live by them. They don't have to consult with anyone in important matters etc. etc. We already know why permissive parenting isn't the best parenting style as it interferes with the child's development of self-control. Too much power is also a bad thing, right?

According to one study, researchers asked adolescent daughters of divorced parents about the relationship with their mothers. Assuming they would hold a stronger bond between them, the findings were completely the opposite. The girls experienced psychological stress that their mothers were always discussing with them the details of their employment hassles, financial worries, negative emotions they had for their ex, and other personal problems (Koerner et al. 2002).

Another research study demonstrated that when parents paid attention and showed affection while at the same time enforced age-appropriate rules, their kids do better.

Another downfall of friendship is that it means treating the child as an adult. Although your child would love that, again, there are many problems with that as well. Parents begin to see kids as their adult therapist and share with them personal lives and sometimes even the intimate confessions about what's going on in their bedroom. This might not be ideal. Basically, as a parent, you should be teaching your child how to have healthy relationships and not lay your problems on them. They don't need to hear that their father and mother are thinking about separating because there is no spark in bed. They don't need to know what new things you two are trying to rekindle it. Let's just settle one thing here: that is TMI!

On the other hand, there have also been supporters of friendship between a child and a parent, suggesting that those bonds are anything but distressing. During a Dutch study in 2013, involving 790 Dutch youngsters, researchers found that kids viewed the parent and child friendship as crucial to their success. They reported happier and stronger bonds built on trust and responsibility. It proposed that when kids grow up in households where they view their parents as their friends instead of just parents, they formed better bonds, had improved self-esteem, and were less likely to indulge in delinquency (Frijns et al. 2013).

According to another study in Sweden, when teenagers were asked which type of parenting they consider beneficial to building their confidence and independence, they rated light-handed parental surveillance higher. Light-handed parenting was basically free-range parenting but with some level of control. The kids wanted to be trusted with the choices they made instead of being told to follow laid out plans. They wanted more freedom with the choice of their careers rather than being told which college they would go to and what profession to choose. All this was only possible if parents stepped back from their role of being parents and became friends with their children.

Hasn't that further confused us? Let's review everything from the beginning and see how parenting has changed over the years from the time when we were kids to now when we have kids.

Parenting in Earlier Times

We remember our upbringing. Every time the image of our childhood runs through our minds, we always see our parents as parents: reserved, authoritative, and stern. Even on days when they were their friendliest, there was still a level of understanding that they were, in fact, our parents and not our friends. They were figures who were to be feared and respected. Just a cold stare from them, and we would feel weak in the knees. If someone had presented the idea of a parent and child friendship back then, we would have laughed it off. It was impossible to think of one!

And if we go further back when our parents were kids during the 1940-1950s, we envision a similar household where mothers were housewives and fathers went to work. The mothers would cook, and the fathers would earn. The mothers would bear children and look after them, whereas the father would only ceremoniously appear friendly. There was a clear difference in the level of respect. They were never to talk back to their parents or try to be too frank. They were to maintain decorum at all times and be disciplined when at the dinner table. Even when watching something funny on the monochromatic TV sets, everyone was expected to stay composed. The households were multigenerational too. There was more than one family generation living together, and everyone pitched in to keep the household running smoothly. The wives and daughters were responsible for the cleaning, washing, ironing, and maintenance of peace in the household. Every day, there was a long list of chores to be completed. Seems quite robotic and stringent, but it was quite beneficial. How so? In terms of behavior and discipline, they seemed more prepared. They just knew what was expected of them and spent their whole lives living up to those expectations. The roles of the parents were somewhat similar to that of matriarchs and patriarchs. The kids were well-mannered and respectful to the elderly, teachers, and other authority figures like the police, doctors, and nurses, etc. You will be shocked that in most families, it was believed that kids should only be seen as prim and proper and not be seen as chaotic.

When baby boomers became parents, they wanted to try out a different approach to parenting. They wanted to be called their child's friend rather than just their parents. They didn't want to be authority figures in their lives. Baby boomers wanted this shift in parenting because they had seen how rigid their parents had been with them and wanted to stay away from that rigidity. They didn't want to be formal with their kids but rather closer and relaxed on the restrictions.

Then came the children of baby boomers (millennials) who wanted their parents to act like adults. We happened to interview a family of two teenagers whose parents approached us for some consultation. The parents were worried about how the kids were average in everything they did and never aced at anything in particular. They wanted to know if there was something wrong that they were doing. So one day, we called in the children to inquire more. During the interview, we realized that the kids had the friendliest set of parents, and yet they were not happy with the way their house ran. They missed having a traditional structure in the household where parents act like parents and give them some space. While questioning the teenagers, all we sensed was chaos. They were over-programmed with too many things to focus on, and they were rendered unable to focus on just a single thing in their lives. They were taking computer classes, learning Spanish, playing the cello, participating in various volunteering programs, and more. Everyone in their household was so busy with their own things that they never had a set time for meals together. They were piled on with homework, tutoring, practice classes, and swimming lessons. They had a strong bond with their parents, but what they really wanted was someone wiser in their choices and more experienced. They wished that their parents would spend more time on their own relationship rather than focusing on the children and the children's future careers. After watching them fail at marriage, the children seemed quite reluctant at their own prospects in the future of finding their soulmate. They wanted some grownups who would offer some routine while making them feel safe and loved. Those children already had many friends but only a single set of parents.

But you can't blame the millennial parents either. All they wanted was a different approach from the one their parents had. They wanted their kids to enjoy further relaxation and live in an open and interactive environment.

However, this is where things started to go a little haywire. The lack of structure in the lives of the children with no set chores or schedules but just an endless focus on extracurricular activities leaves kids tired and unprepared for the world. We see the shifting paradigm where kids cocoon back into their parent's basements as they find it difficult to face responsibilities that come with adulthood. They fail at following orders, establishing independence, lack the capacity to build interpersonal relationships, and want someone to look up to. They feel unfit for the world. No doubt, they are highly empathetic, care about their surroundings, climate, health, and people more than their parents ever did, but due to the lack of an authority figure they could look up to, they keep tumbling down the stairs to success.

Friend or Disciplinarian? What Should it Be?

The relationship between the two has stood the test of time. However, when it comes to raising a child, it is isn't just black or white. We can't ignore that neither of these is perfect parenting styles as we have viewed the flaws of both. So what if we can propose something in between these two? Perhaps, a third type to raise emotionally intelligent and disciplined kids? Because let's face it, as parents, we will never stop caring about them, and most of the time, also give in to their demands and requests. We just want to see them happy and doing well. So we keep reading books, listening to parenting experts, seeking counseling, and implementing strategies to ensure we raise them to be wise, confident, and happy.

To answer the question, let's try to look at it with an example. Imagine your teenager comes up to you and tells you that he has plans with his friends and will, therefore, be staying the night at his friend's place. He then asks if you are okay with it or not.

The first thing to note here is that the kid has just come to inform and not seek permission. This shows that the kid knows that his parents trust him and will have no problem with the stayover. This also means that they are on pleasant terms with each other. But this also doesn't mean that there is a lack of structure in the house as the kid then asks if the parent is ok with the stay over or not.

This is a middle ground that we want to create. As parents, all we want for our kids is that they will come up to us whenever they want to discuss whatever they want. However, they also know about the boundaries there are. Being too friendly with them can be mistaken for complete freedom without any limits. Without these parental limits, there is a possibility that your child might feel that there is no need to seek advice from an adult about some decision that isn't age-appropriate. Their lack of judgment can make them end up in jail. They may not have done something to get arrested but maybe helped someone who was trouble all along and got pinned with them in jail. So, although it is best to encourage kids to be self-reliant, parents shouldn't hand them over all the power. This is also one reason why it is so important to have some direction and discipline in their lives.

On the one hand, you should not be so harsh with them that they can't wait to cut all ties from you once they are 18 and on the other, you don't want to be too friendly with them to the point where they think they are their own god and do whatever they want.

According to Anna Freud, the role a parent plays is that of a mother bird. Ever noticed how she pushes her little ones from the nest so that they can learn to fly? This is called mentorship. It is guiding them to create a space for themselves in the world but with some direction. It is about nudging them to become independent but making that transition gradually. The bird doesn't leave the child on its own. She also shows them by examples of how to eat, hunt, and fly. As a parent, you also need to find that balance in your relationship. You don't have to be a friend or a disciplinarian but rather a coach that they can come to with all their problems because they see you as wiser and authoritative.

Becoming a Mentor and Mentorship

So how can you attain this title in between a disciplinarian and a friend? Being a mentor has its own set of rules. New or old, all parents must try to restore a balance. Below are some valuable insights into becoming a mentor for your kids and helping them pave their way to emotional well-being and success.

The first step involves integrity. No mentor can do without it. You have to have a strong character as that is what determines how well or poorly you will raise your children. Even when you think that your children aren't paying attention or around, present yourself in good character. They are always learning, and you don't want them to be learning things that aren't good. Therefore, in order to become their guide and mentor, acting like one is essential. The thought behind this is that kids mirror their parents. They are their first teachers. So you have to set a good example for them to follow.

The next step is to stay committed. Kids detest the idea of forgotten promises. They don't want a promise maker but rather a promise keeper. Since you want to take up the role of mentorship, you have to ensure that your mentees feel it too. Be a parent that keeps their words. Your kids consider you a role model, so ensure that they know that you are someone who says what they mean and means what they say. If you want them to come to you for guidance and direction, you have to make yourself seem reliable in the first place.

The third step involves being compassionate. As a parent, your ultimate goal should be able to create a safe space for your kids so that they don't hide from you. They should come to you to share things. You need to create an environment where they feel safe to learn and grow. Although you would hate to correct them at times, you must let them know that you and they are on the same team. This is the part where you teach them good values with love and discipline.

Next comes coaching. A good mentor is no less than a coach who makes it their goal to work on them and make them a star. Keep in mind that your wisdom is what will guide them. However, you can only teach them what you know, which is why it is important that you not only tell them how you overcame the biggest obstacles in your life but actually show them too. And hope they pick up something from your expertise and wisdom.

What follows is earning respect. Any good mentor would know that it is different than bending the knee. It has to come from the heart. Your kids should respect you without you asking for it. How can you earn their respect? By being transparent and honest with them at all times. If you think that the idea they came up with for a science project has many loopholes, you have to kindly tell them your opinion and help them improve on their ideas. You shouldn't set your children up for failure when you know you could have helped them succeed. This does not mean that you should not let your children fail at all but help them succeed enough to build their self-confidence and problem-solving skills. If they trust and show reliance on you, you have to be reliable and be there for them. Be open to discuss the nitty-gritty of things and have a difficult conversation, not just the good parts. Talk about your personal failure and mistakes, but also tell them how you coped with them. This way, you will be able to connect with them on a deeper level because they will see that you aren't perfect either and thus relate to you better.

Then, you have to stay committed and devoted to them. They have to see you as someone they can depend on at all times and not just when you are in a good mood. Mentorship is all about maintaining relationships. Staying in constant contact with your children is another important pillar of parenting. This doesn't mean that you have to poke your nose into everything they are doing but also not turn a blind eye on them. Parenting is not a part-time duty. You are in it for a lifetime. Thus, always be there for them when they need you.

Finally, we have communication. Communication is an important aspect of bridging between the two distinctive parenting types. We have to be careful of the vocabulary we use around them. Your communications should be welcoming but not too frank. There should be a thin line of respect in between. Secondly, this also means that as their mentor, you have to know what questions to ask them. Try to empower them but also hold them accountable when needed.

Chapter 7: A Teen Rebel in the House. Is Parenting with Purpose Still Possible?

At times, parenting can be daunting, especially when your kid enters the golden years of his/her life, aka the teen ages. Teenage is the age where kids can cause mental exhaustion. It is the time for emotional intensity, identity development, risk-taking, rapid brain growth, vitality, and novelty seeking. They have passed the age where they relied on you for everything. They are becoming more and more independent, rebellious, and developing self-esteem issues. Since most kids hit puberty during these years, they can be extra cranky, emotional, or shy about their appearance.

So if you have a kid just reaching the phase, be prepared to be ignored, judged, and considered an old man/woman because, apparently, you know nothing. A little harsh, we know!

But it doesn't have to look this gloomy. If parenting has been done right, they should be the greatest and brightest stars in the room with good values, discipline, enlightenment, and emotional intelligence.

How Teenagers Differ from Toddlers and Adults

Parenting a toddler or a preschooler is one thing. Dealing with a teenager is a completely different ball game. Teenagers are entering a challenging phase of life that often makes them rebellious, moody, and irrational. Doing mindful parenting with a teen rebel in the house will take your efforts to a whole new level. But before we discuss all that, how about taking a look at the differences between them and adults?

Risky Behavior

We all remember the stupid things we did when we were teenagers. From the roller skating to rash driving, yes, we have done it all. Now that we look back, we wonder why we took so many risks in life. Well, research has some clarification. When we are in our teen years, we rarely think things through as our mind is bombarded with so much new information and hormonal zest and zeal. We want to act cooler by attempting things others would think twice before doing. Their brains think things through quickly without fully considering the whole picture. The frontal lobe in the brain that is responsible for the majority of the decision-making we do in our lives isn't fully connected with the other brain regions. Thus, when we are teenagers, we think faster and come to a decision sooner than adults. Did you know that a teen's brain takes less than 170 milliseconds to decide whether they want to do something or not? Certainly, no risk-involving activity takes this little thinking.

Overly Emotional

How many times have we told our teenage sons and daughters to get over something? Here's an eye-opener. They aren't purposely trying to be hard to handle. They aren't drama queens either. Studies show that the reason why teens can be so emotional over little things is that they interpret facial expressions and vocal inflection differently. When shown an image of a woman's expressions, 50% of the teenage responders said that she looked fearful. The other 50% was divided between anger and sadness. Then, researchers showed them some more pictures after hooking up their brains to an MRI machine.

Later, some adults were called in for the same inspection. Researchers were astonished to find that teenagers and adults used two very different regions of their brains to interpret the emotions on the face of the woman. The adults were using the part that controlled reason and logic, whereas the teenagers were using the amygdala, the part that regulates emotions. This meant that your kids might be interpreting an emotion you are going through as something entirely different.

Giving Into Peer Pressure

Imagine you are in a book club where everyone loves to read the same book as you. You all have the same genre favorites, and whenever you all get together to discuss it, the joy is indescribable. You follow what your friends read and vice versa. Now imagine a gathering involving teenagers who have the adrenaline pumping in their veins. They are all as excited as the other to be part of a group. Peer pressure might lead a group of teenagers in bad directions and encourage them to participate in risky behaviors. No wonder we are told to have good company as the influences of our friends do brush off on us too. When teenagers become adults, that excitement to try new things is outgrown. Their brain and ability to make a sound judgment is more well developed. Hence, they enter a calmer and more mature stage.

Research shows that when we are with our friends, our ability to make decisions changes. This was visible during an MRI scan on both adults and teens. The findings revealed that the brains of both adults and teenagers reacted differently in the company of their friends. The findings also proposed that we were less likely to take risks when alone as compared to when we knew our friends were watching us. So basically, part of their show of risky behavior is due to the fact that they are being watched. The central part of their brain that regulates reward and pleasure lights up too. They want to be praised as well. Remember the 170 milliseconds we talked about earlier? That thinking time combines with our need for praise. So teenagers are fighting two very different but inviting things before deciding the worthiness of a risk.

They Get Dumb

Not long ago, you wouldn't stop gloating about how smart your child is, how quickly they pick up on things, how cleverly they solved problems, etc. but as they head for their teen years, you notice them losing that interest in life, and their grades also seem to decline. They go from being an A+ student to a B- or worse. So what went wrong? Was it your parenting to blame?

Well, not you, but the changes in their brains. Decades ago, researchers believed that IQ was something that remained constant throughout one's life. But recent studies show that isn't the whole truth. Our IQ fluctuates in adolescence, which could be the reason behind your child's intellectual decline.

Remember the grey matter we talked about earlier? When we are in infancy, the grey matter has numerous synapses that help the brain retain and process information. But as we grow older, our brain kills off bits that are no longer required. It's like the disk cleanup app on your phone that asks you to delete apps you never or rarely use to make some space for the important stuff.

And it makes sense. After all, why should the brain waste energy retain information that is no longer required? Do you remember all the formulas we did in math when we were young? Since we never applied them in our practical lives, our brains killed off those bits of information to create space for new information to be processed.

The same happens with teenagers. They forget things they learned when they were young. For example, a child might be bilingual as a toddler; however, as they became adult, they might lose a language due to lack of use and practice.

Poor Concentration

One of the many reasons teenagers find academics so tough is because their mind isn't developed enough to concentrate better. Although their bodies are changing shape rapidly, their mind, not as fast. Due to the changes happening in the brain, it is still in a transitional state from adolescence to teens. When the activity of their brain was monitored during an assigned task, the researchers discovered a lot of grey matter in the frontal lobe. It was more than what was considered normal for an adult. The reason that happened was that teenagers tried to take in so much information at once that they overloaded their systems. It happens with us too. When we are occupied with more than one thing at a time, we aren't able to focus on anything solely. The same happens when we try to multitask. Although we are doing more things, our attention to each is a bare minimum. This is one reason why single-tasking is becoming the new hype recently.

Understanding Parenting with Purpose for Teenagers

Parenting with purpose, aka mindful parenting, changes its meaning when teenagers are involved. It becomes more direct, guided, and important as this is that crucial age where there is most retaliation against conflicting ideas. However, since it is going to be hard for both the parent and the child to guide and listen, it has to start with the right mindset. Parents need to outline their objectives, manage their own emotions and actions before they expect their kids to. Have you ever traveled via an airplane? Do you notice how the flight attendant always tells us to wear our oxygen mask first and then move onto placing it on our kids and the elderly?

It is because our mental and emotional health has to be in a stable condition before we preach to others. We have to become role models for our kids so that they follow in our steps. To teach them how to regulate their emotions, you have to first regulate your own. Why? Because you can't parent well when you feel sick, stressed out, distracted, or overwhelmed yourself.

First, to get a few things straight: parenting with purpose doesn't mean being the perfect parent. You, too, can have bad days or be emotional. You might think that your parenting sucks when you see other kids behaving well and your child eating with their hands instead of a fork, but it isn't something you can ever fail at as long as you are doing the best you can do for who you are at that moment. When a bad day gets to you, give yourself a little grace. You are doing better than you think!

Even if you fail, pick yourself up and find the opportunity to do better and try again.

Mindful parenting requires that you bring your A-game to the table when it comes to handling your emotions. You can't let them hijack your parenting when they go out of control. It involves letting go of the grudges that are weighing you down and focusing on the present. It involves acceptance of what's going on before trying to ignore or change it.

When you try to become a mindful parent, you need to be attentive to your feelings. It often gets mistaken for having a calm attitude, but you can be angry, sad, disappointed, or upset too. There is no running away from negative emotions; however, becoming victimized by them is where you fail. You need to act mindfully, not mindlessly.

Some benefits of mindful parenting include becoming responsive to your child's emotions and yours. You tend to be more forgiving and less critical of your children's choices and opinions. You learn how to control impulsive reactions and not give in to them as it doesn't set a good example for them to follow. Most importantly, the relationship between you and your children improves drastically.

Using Mindful Parenting with Teenagers

When the ultimate goal is to have cohesive relationships, there is a lot that the parents can learn and implement that resonates with the child's brain development. If we have to tell you one simple knowledge to bridge that gap between a parent and child using mindfulness, it would be this: *Honor the Differences!*

Yes, it is just that. You see, we keep focusing on the wrong things. Every other message in the book tells us to look for the similarities and cultivate the relationship using that. But it is the opposite. You have to honor the differences and try to find a middle ground there. Otherwise, they will keep resisting you as they will see you as someone that doesn't support their unique opinions and ideas. So work on what's not right as a start and see where you two can connect.

Let's look at an example for a better understanding. Your child comes home to you all excited and enthusiastic about something. Upon inquiry, they tell you that they found a little butterfly in the backyard and would like to keep it. A non-integrated response would be something like this: don't bring it into the house.

What you did here is that you missed an opportunity to bond and be present. Of course, they have a different opinion than yours as they would like to take in the butterfly, but your disapproval dishonors that. A better response would have been this: Really, a butterfly? Oh, you must be so excited. Let's see what it looks like!

Notice the visible difference in these two sentences. You still haven't agreed to take in the butterfly, but you have shown enthusiasm in them and have sided with them on the idea.

You might be thinking that we are fools to suggest that, but think about it for a minute. The kid will probably outgrow their obsession for it and might themselves free them in a day or two as they get busy with their studies and homework. So basically, you have bonded with them as well as honored their decision. You may have already been placed on the podium for the best parent.

Some other helpful ways to further deepen that bond with mindful parenting involves the following.

Take a Deep Breath

We make our kids rush things. We want them to get in the car instantly, get dressed on time, eat and sleep on time, etc. Although all these are an essential part of parenting, pushing them too often and over everything in their lives can create a rift between the two of you. They may feel like a prisoner or that they are living under a dictatorship. How does that affect you? It affects you when they stop responding to your demands positively. Let's just take their morning routine, for instance. How many times do you yell at them for not getting up or dressing earlier, or not eating their breakfast fast enough?

Take a deep breath and let them take one too. Instead of rushing them, be better at time management. They have every right to feel distant or agitated when they find you on their nerves all the time. So practice mindfulness by managing things and routines better. You have a problem with them waking up late, how about talking about rescheduling the wake-up time 15-20 minutes earlier? Of course, it will take some time for implementation, but you will get there.

Listen Actively

Be an active listener, and that means no talking and only listening. It is very hard for parents to become active listeners. First, they love their child beyond everything, so watching them stressed out and not wrapping them into a tight hug is hard. Second, they want to keep their child safe. So the minute they sense danger, they start sharing their opinions or even get aggressive. Third, they think that their children are still babies and thus can't stop themselves from looking after them.

But it sends them the wrong signal, and you might miss out on the opportunity to have another such heart-to-heart conversation with them if you keep interrupting them with your gestures and wisdom. Maybe they don't need that. Maybe they just want to be heard by someone. So wait until they ask you for your opinion. If they don't, let them finish and wait for a better time to offer them.

Be Attentive to your Reactions

Pay attention to your own responses to certain situations. If they see you stressed out, angry or frustrated, they are going to react the same when facing a similar situation. If you have the habit of getting aggravated over a little thing instantly, then they are going to view it as an acceptable response to minor issues that come up in their daily life. If they are in the same room as you and you feel angry over something, don't lash out. Keep your cool until you are calm. Avoid reacting or depicting negative emotions in front of them.

Even when the bad gets worse, you have to maintain a degree of levelheadedness and poise because your kids are watching you. Besides, you are an adult. You should be better at handling nuisances better than your child. Outside of parenting, you have dealt with many greater problems than the ones presented by your little humans. As a parent, you overcame countless of sleepless nights. You kept them alive and safe from harm. You take care of them when they are sick. The fact that you are reading this book means that you overcame 100% of the difficult times you had in life. What makes you doubt that you won't be able to handle the current situation you are in?

If you really cannot manage the negative emotions in a certain situation, one way to handle this is to remove yourself from the room. If you think that your emotions need a proper venting out and cool down, do it where your children are not present.

Don't Aim for Perfectionism

Aiming for perfection will get you nowhere and can be detrimental. No one can't be the epitome of perfection at all times. Teenagers who grow up in households where they see their parents being perfect at everything try to do the same. This leaves the children with unrealistic expectations, and they begin to lose their confidence when they don't meet the unrealistic expectations they set for themselves. As a parent, you don't want your children to chase perfection. You want them to be the best versions of themselves and live a fulfilled life.

Starting with yourself, stop beating yourself over things that aren't in your control. You don't want them to do the same. So in place of aiming for perfection, aim for improvement and progress in all areas of you and your children's lives.

Finally, you have to understand that as hard as it is for you to act like a parent, it is equally hard for the teen to act like a grownup. They are in the midst of identity development and more confused than you when you first held them in your arms and didn't know what to do. This is where incorporating mindfulness comes into play. It allows you to have an open mind, focus on the present, and use strategies that help them make the transition from an adolescent to a teenager, minus all the drama.

Chapter 8: Applying Parenting with Purpose to Different Scenarios

Think of this chapter as a roundup of all that we have discussed earlier in the book, just consolidated into one chapter. This is meant to tie everything that we have covered in various places – sometimes briefly and other times in great depth. Since the goal of this book was to parent with purpose, we will explore how to do so in various challenging situations parents face when dealing with toddlers or teenagers.

The rules haven't changed. We still want to raise our children well-mannered and emotionally intelligent using mindful techniques. Let's start with the most obvious and prevalent ones among toddlers:

Public Temper Tantrums

A temper tantrum is like fire—once it starts, it is hard to put out. It is nature's way of setting off your emotional alarm, and the worst part, there is no snooze button. Tantrums are an age-appropriate phenomenon most common among toddlers and adolescents. Therefore, acting quickly to prevent them from becoming more aggressive and wild should be our first goal on the list.

- First up, we have acknowledgment, which means that you understand that it is happening. This is for the parents to mentally prepare themselves for it so that their brains can come up with better ideas to tackle it. This will prevent you from getting emotionally stormed. Labeling it as a tantrum will activate certain regions in your brain, which will allow you to come up with better ideas and techniques.
- The very first idea should be exiting the place and taking the tantrum somewhere private if it's happening in the middle of a busy road or shop.
- Second, you should let them know that you know how they are feeling. This involves acknowledging their feelings and comforting them a little by saying that you understand what they are going through and why they are acting out. Show empathy and tell them that you are on their side.
- Next, you can try distracting them with something else. Distractions mostly work for toddlers with limited

understanding of diversions. So it can be a hit or miss, depending on the age of your child. When kids feel stressed out over something, they momentarily lose the capacity to think wisely, which is exactly what we need to work on. Divert them with things they are interested in, such as saying, "Oh, look at that car. It looks so dirty. It looks like no one has cleaned it for months."

- If distraction does not work, let your kids ride out their emotions. Research shows that doing nothing can be the best way to deal with tantrums. Do not worry about what other people around you might think. And do not give in to what your child wants to try to resolve the situation. This can be quite hard, but having a firm limit is part of positive discipline.

- One good way to deal with a tantrum is to prevent it from happening in the first place. Telling your children what's going on is a good start. When a child knows what to expect, they are less likely to be frustrated when something happens. For example, if you are at your friend's house and your child has access to your friend's child's toys, tell your child that the toys are not for them to keep. Say something like, "Looks like you are having a lot of fun with these toys. You can play with them while we are here, but we will have to return the toys to the basket when we leave, so Amelia (your friend's kid) can play with them later" or "We will be leaving in 15 minutes. Please get ready."

- Always be prepared. Kids often have a meltdown when they are tired, hungry, or bored. When you run errands with your kid, make sure to pack some biscuits, fruit bars, a water bottle, and some toys, like stickers, stuffed animals, or coloring books. Yes, this will make your bag or purse bulkier, but I think you would agree that a bulky purse is easier to deal with than a tantrum.

Hitting and Slapping Siblings, Parents and Other Kids

Before rushing towards them with an angry or worried expression on your face, try to understand why they are so keen on hitting others. Do they feel jealous? Do they feel unloved? Are they learning it via wrong exposure to TV or games? All these are questions you need to ask yourself before yelling or shouting at them to stop. It might just be all an act to get your attention, which is exactly what they are getting as a response.

- Start with accepting their feelings. If they are feeling angry or agitated, tell them that you acknowledge it. Once they know that you two are on the same page and that the parent is able to accept and respond calmly to the child's emotion, this will give the child a better chance of calming down. If they are old enough to answer, ask them what is bothering them, and why they are hitting or slapping. Is it out of jealousy or over something they wanted to be done?

- Next, you need to teach them that such behavior isn't appreciated but in a subtle way. They shouldn't feel like they are being preached to or coached as it will further agitate them. Give them reasons why they need to stop. Tell them how it hurts others when you hit them or how it makes you feel upset.

- Since they will still be dealing with negative emotions, tell them how to get it all out in a positive manner. For instance, instead of hitting, they can tell you that they are angry by using their words, writing their feelings on papers, or going to their room until they feel better. Basically, provide them with options that don't involve hitting, slapping, or biting.

Safety and the Enforcement of Safety Rules (playing with matches, crossing the street, talking to strangers)

This is a highly recommended parenting essential that kids should learn at an early age to prevent many in-house incidents from happening. Below are some strategies you can use.

- Use positivity instead of fear to tell them what's allowed and what isn't. Use positive words when instructing them on how they shouldn't pick up a knife from the table or light a match stick.

- Be subtle but stern on how crucial it is for you that they understand the rules you want in place. Ensure that you get a nod from them so that you know they hear you. Your tone should be slightly bossy, as you want them to see the rules as rules and not mere suggestions.

- Add solid reasoning as to why the rule is important to follow.

- Have some clearly-communicated consequences if you find them doing any of the non-doable things. They don't have to be harsh in general, just things that they would rather not have happening to them. An example of this can be getting grounded or not watching their favorite cartoons for a day.

- Since kids have the habit of forgetting things or giving in to the temptation of trying, you have to keep reviewing the rules from time to time so that they don't accidentally break them.

- To prevent this from happening, you can place the list of safety measures in an accessible place, so there are little chances that they would miss seeing it.

- Set a good example for them to follow. If they see you crossing the road without inspecting the traffic on either side, they are going to do the same. It's just that simple. Therefore, be their ideal as they look up to you for guidance.

Dining and Meal Tantrums

Mealtimes can be hard to handle as kids have varying tastes in food. Sometimes, they will be all too excited to finish a plate of boiled peas, and other times, they won't even touch them. Some days, they will eat everything there is and others will spend time playing with the food. So what is the right way to approach them with positive parenting? Take a look below.

- To begin with, some kids will always have a problem with eating things you want them to eat. They just are weird that way. And don't even get us started on the things we don't want them to eat. They are after those like a monster. Aim for a balance between healthy and fun foods. Start with the healthy first and then finish off with something of their choice. However, make it a point to let them know that the only way they will be able to enjoy the fun food is if they finish the healthy first.

- Second, teach them how to eat mindfully. Ask them to use their senses to describe the food. Ask them how it looks, what it smells like, is its texture smooth or crunchy, or if they can smell the spices or not. They should be made aware of everything that's on their plate, and this is the best way to do so.

- Give them a comfortable place at the dinner table. Make it seem like an important one so that they can feel like an adult. Let them have their cutlery and don't chop their food into small chunks unless they ask you to.

- To convince them to eat healthy, concoct stories about the food. Tell them where it is grown, who cuts and makes it, how it gets shipped to stores, etc. The more they know about something, the more excited they will be to consume it.

Getting Dressed Tantrums

Isn't that a struggle for both the parent and the child? Yes, tell us about it! One minute they want to wear a shirt with an astronaut on it and the next, they are into fish. There is no telling or predicting with kids when it comes to dressing them. But this isn't the point where things get hard. Things get hard when they start school or nursery, and you have to wake them up every morning to get dressed on time. It is important that your tiny human starts their day glad and happy as it sets the tone for their mood throughout the day. If they are cranky first thing in the morning, there is little chance that their mood will improve during the day. So first things first, ensure that they get a good night's sleep and have no reason to be groggy the next day. Depending on the age group your child belongs to, allow them to enjoy sound sleep for 10-12 hours. Then throw in some short naps during the day to keep their brain refreshed.

- Once they are up, don't run after them like a coach in a football game. Don't tell them to hurry up, brush their teeth, get dressed, comb their hair, or tie their laces. They hate being directed, and you know that too well. Continuing to stand over their heads, judging them on their effort will only crank up the craziness meter.

- Use the first 15 to 20 minutes to connect and cuddle with them. Relationships should always come first, routines later. If you want to stay connected, snuggles are the best way to do that. It will also give your little one some time to gather their thoughts and mentally prepare themselves to get up and dressed.

- Limit excessive talking for later once they are out for breakfast. It also hinders the organization and process of dressing.

- Keep your choices limited if they need your help dressing. Just lay out what you want them to wear, don't ask if they would like to have cereal or pancakes, or if they would like to wear sneakers or sandals. Multiple choices make their brains go into a tailspin.

- Lastly, don't make it a battle worth fighting over if they just want to go out in their pajamas. They might want to try it once or twice. If the behavior persists, get some pajamas that go well as pants or trousers too. That way, it won't look like they just climbed out of bed and into the daycare.

Whiny Behavior, Begging and Threatening to Get Their Way

Again, something that is embarrassing for the parent and others to witness. Some undisciplined kids use this tactic, hoping they would get their way and convince their parents to listen to them. When they notice how stressed it is making you feel, they amp up the drama and whine some more. If, like most parents, you have been through such a humiliating sight where you begin to reevaluate all your teachings, here is how you are going to handle this and make it stop once and for all.

- First up, don't feel humiliated or focus your attention on what others are thinking about you or your parenting. Right now, the only point of focus should be your child. Acknowledge what is happening at that moment and think about ways to calm them down. Even if the first thing that comes to your mind is grabbing them and exiting the store, do that! Just don't let others get to you. You are doing great. If you have a stronger heart, try the next one on the list.

- Make them see that it isn't bothering you. The #1 reason why kids whine or get noisy is that they know it gets your attention. You offer them a payoff. Remove that, and they will stop viewing it as a way to have your attention. At first, it will get more annoying and dramatic, but gradually this behavior will be cut back. Do not give them negative attention.

- Third, provide warning and make that the end of the conversation. Use an "if…then statement" and be prepared to follow through. If your child doesn't comply, follow through with the consequences. Do not give multiple warnings as this would decrease the gravity of your words. Make it clear that when their behavior crosses the line, it won't be tolerated. Be consistent with your discipline. Being consistent is difficult and exhausting, but it is the key to positive parenting.

- When the unwanted behavior stop, offer positive attention. Praise your child when they behave the way you want. You can say something like, "I like the way you talk to me nicely right now or play with your sister quietly right now."

- Finally, you may try reverse psychology. Reverse psychology can be effective; however, it can also do more harm than good. This technique should be used sparingly and as the last resource when all other methods are exhausted. One way to do this offer them a choice, so the child feels like they have some power in the situation. For example, if they refuse to eat vegetables, say, "OK, would you rather eat cabbage or green beans?" Another way is to challenge them instead of giving them orders, such as "I bet you can't be as quiet as your little brother," or "I bet I can finish these vegetables before I can." You may also try to create a picture in your children's mind to reinforce that negative behavior, such as whining and pestering, is unlikeable. Basically, take the negative aspect of something and tell your kid that they are doing that behavior. Then, the child (hopefully) will try to act the opposite. In this case, tell your child that nobody likes being around whining and crying kids. Then ask them if they are trying to make people dislike them by crying and whining. Humans have a natural tendency to want to be liked and accepted. Hence, this will make them think twice before whining and crying. However, be cautious with this technique because reverse psychology can harm your child's self-esteem and cause the feeling of guilt if used incorrectly.

Conclusion

Parenting isn't simple math. Many variables come into play. Sometimes, these variables are controllable and other times not so. As a parent, our goal is to solve the mysteries and reach a conclusion – one that satisfies us inside and out. We want to be able to raise our heads with pride and show the world we haven't succumbed to the uncontrollable variables because we have learned to solve them too.

This book is your guide to solving those uncontrollable and unexpected variables that pop up unannounced, sometimes in the middle of a grocery store, and other times in the bathroom while bathing them.

If we go back and look at the actual problem, it was to instill good habits and values in kids and raise them to be conscious, disciplined, and emotionally intelligent to regulate their emotions better. The easily solvable variables we had were the things we already knew – thanks to our own childhood – and then some weren't too predictable, such as misbehavior, reluctance, and the will to counteract everything. However, when we introduced parenting with purpose into the equation, we noticed how simple it was to control these variables and reach our desired values. We started with what it was and then later delved into the many parameters it holds. We talked about the working of the human brain and how it differs from that of an adult. After that, we assessed our practices in chapter 3. We saw what style of parenting we have and how it can be improved so that we can be a better parent.

Then we moved on to discussing why kids misbehave and what the different approaches are to dealing with it. We also had a detailed look at how behaviors influence our actions. Following that, we talked about emotional intelligence and what it meant to raise kids based on that philosophy.

In the next chapter, we learned of the behavioral as well as physical changes an adolescent goes into when they become teenagers and how to help them navigate their way through the many changes they are experiencing. Finally, we looked at whether or not being a friend to our kids was what they needed and whether a balance between a disciplinarian and a friend can be created. Turns out, a combination of both in the form of mentorship is what promises the best result.

Following that quick roundup of the book, we hope that you found the answers to your problems in it. We hope that it helps you find your way through the many obstacles that come with parenting. As parenting counselors, we want our clients to be able to deal with the issues they face with parenting, especially if it's the first child in their family. Sometimes we just feel like giving up altogether, but that is no solution. As you must have noticed in chapter eight, every problem has a solution that doesn't involve fear, punishments, or time-outs. The goal is to help them understand their emotional outbursts on their own. They don't need punishments to learn that. They need counseling, guidance, and mentorship. They want someone they can look up to for advice. So, be there for them.

And even if you feel like failing, keep in mind that you have your whole life to rectify the mistakes. You will get countless chances, the only important thing to keep in mind is this: are you willing to rectify?

Help Others Discover Parenting With Purpose

Thank you for reading our book. We hope you enjoyed it as much as we enjoyed writing it. If you do enjoy this book and find it helpful in any ways, please consider leaving a review. Even just a few words will help others decide if the book is right for them.

Leave review at: https://tinyurl.com/PWP-reviews

Join our 30-Day Positive Parenting Challenge

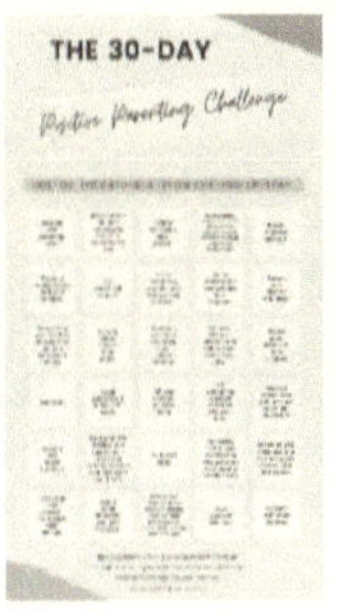

Many of life's greatest lessons are best learned through experience. Like all other skills, parenting takes practice. This 30-day challenge is designed to help you apply what you learn in this book and become the best version of parent you can be!

Ready to take on the challenge?

Visit this link: https://tinyurl.com/PWP-freegift

References

5 Steps To Nurture Emotional Intelligence in Your Child. (n.d.). Retrieved December 19, 2019, from https://www.ahaparenting.com/parenting-tools/emotional-intelligence/steps-to-encourage

American SPCC. (2019, February 12). What is Positive Discipline? Retrieved December 19, 2019, from https://americanspcc.org/2019/02/12/what-is-positive-discipline/

American Psychological Organization. (n.d.). Parenting Styles. Retrieved December 19, 2019, from https://www.apa.org/act/resources/fact-sheets/parenting-styles

Association for Psychological Science. (2012, July 7). Inside a Child's Mind — Research Findings from Psychological Science. Retrieved December 19, 2019, from https://www.psychologicalscience.org/news/releases/inside-a-childs-mind-research-findings-from-psychological-science.html

Ceder, J. (2017, October 19). Mindful Parenting: How to Respond Instead of React. Retrieved December 19, 2019, from https://www.huffpost.com/entry/mindful-parenting-how-to-respond-instead-of-react_b_59e8c431e4b0153c4c3ec5be

Committee on Developments in the Science of Learning with additional material from the Committee on Learning Research and Educational Practice, National Research Council. (n.d.). Read "How People Learn: Brain, Mind, Experience, and School: Expanded Edition" at NAP.edu. Retrieved December 19, 2019, from https://www.nap.edu/read/9853/chapter/7

Dewar PhD, G. (2018, February 28). Parenting styles: An evidence-based guide. Retrieved December 19, 2019, from https://www.parentingscience.com/parenting-styles.html

Dewar, G. (n.d.). Should parents be friends with their kids? Retrieved December 19, 2019, from https://www.parentingscience.com/parents-be-friends.html

Ferguson, C. J. (2013). Spanking, corporal punishment and negative long-term outcomes: a meta-analytic review of longitudinal studies. Clinical Psychology Review, 196-208.

Garber, J., Robinson, N. S., & Valentiner, D. (1997). The Relation Between Parenting and Adolescent Depression: Self-Worth as a Mediator. Journal of Adolescent Research, 12–33.

Gershoff, E. T., & Grogan-Kaylor, A. (2016). Spanking and child outcomes: Old controversies and new meta-analyses. Journal of Family Psychology, 453–469.

Hamilton, L. (2016, June 10). The dawn (and rewards) of helicopter parenting. (K. Hartnett, Interviewer)

Hotchkin, K. (2017, September 21). 5 Easy Ways to Parent with Purpose. Retrieved from https://healthblog.uofmhealth.org/health-management/5-easy-ways-to-parent-purpose

Kelly. (2019, March 7). When your toddler acts defiant, here are the hidden reasons why. Retrieved from https://happyyouhappyfamily.com/toddler-brain/

Koerner SS, Wallace S, Lehman SJ, and Raymond M. 2002. Mother-to-Daughter Disclosure After Divorce: Are There Costs and Benefits? Journal of Child and Family Studies 11(4): 1062-1024 CBS News. (2010, August 18). Should You Be Friends With Your Kids? Retrieved from https://www.cbsnews.com/news/should-you-be-friends-with-your-kids/

Kim, J. (2009). Type-specific intergenerational transmission of neglectful and physically abusive parenting behaviors among young parents. Children and Youth Services Review, 761-767.

Lonczak, H. (2019, July 4). What is Positive Parenting? A Look at the Research and Benefits. Retrieved from https://positivepsychology.com/positive-parenting/

Miller, P. M., & Commons, M. L. (2010). The Benefits of Attachment Parenting for Infants and Children: A Behavioral Developmental View. Behavioral Development Bulletin, 1-14.

Moore, C. (2019, August 1). Is Emotional Intelligence Relevant for Kids? (Games, Cartoons + Toys). Retrieved December 19, 2019, from https://positivepsychology.com/emotional-intelligence-for-kids/

Monroe, J. (2019, May 1). A Q&A with Dr. Dan Siegel: Raising Healthy Teens with Mindful... Retrieved December 19, 2019, from https://www.newportacademy.com/resources/expert-qa/mindful-parenting/

Moore, K. A., Kinghorn, A., & Bandy, T. (2011). Parental Relationship Quality and Child Outcomes Across Subgroups. Child Trends Research Brief.

Pelini, S. (2018, August 16). 3 things to ban from your kid's diet to calm anxiety and hyperactivity. From Raising Independent Kids: https://raising-independent-kids.com/3-things-ban-kids-diet-calm-anxiety-hyperactivity/

Raising an Emotionally Intelligent Child, Ages 1 to 3. (2019, January 1). Retrieved December 19, 2019, from https://consumer.healthday.com/encyclopedia/children-s-health-10/child-development-news-124/raising-an-emotionally-intelligent-child-ages-1-to-3-646450.html

Sarkadi, A., Kristiansson, R., Oberklaid, F., & Bremberg, S. (2007). Fathers' involvement and children's developmental outcomes: a systematic review of longitudinal studies. Acta Paediatrica, 153-158.

Slobin, S. (2017, November 27). One paragraph disproves that helicopter parenting is a modern phenomenon. From Quartz: https://qz.com/1138189/helicopter-parenting-isnt-a-modern-phenomenon/

Spokane Regional Health District. (n.d.). What Is Positive Discipline. Retrieved from https://srhd.org/media/documents/What20is20Positive20Discipline1.pdf

Steinberg, L. (2001). We know some things: Parent–adolescent relationships in retrospect and prospect. Journal of Research on Adolescence, 1–19.

Tech Insider. (2016, May 25). Science says parents of unsuccessful kids could have these 9 things in common. Retrieved December 19, 2019, from https://www.businessinsider.com/parenting-techniques-unsuccessful-children-2016-5?international=true&r=US&IR=T

This Is How To Raise Emotionally Intelligent Kids: 5 Secrets From Research. (n.d.). Retrieved from https://www.bakadesuyo.com/2018/09/emotionally-intelligent-kids/

Wang, M.-T., & Kenny, S. (2014). Longitudinal Links Between Fathers' and Mothers' Harsh Verbal Discipline And Adolescents' Conduct Problems and Depressive Symptoms. Child Development, 908–923.

Worthen, B. (2012, September 29). The Perils of Texting While Parenting. From The Wall Street Journal: https://www.wsj.com/articles/SB10000872396390444772404577589683644202996

Zimmerman, F., Christakis, D. A., & Meltzoff, A. N. (2007). Associations between Media Viewing and Language Development in Children Under Age 2 Years. The Journal of Pediatrics, 364-368.

Mindful Habits for Better Parents

*How to Stop Losing Your Sh*t and Start Owning Parenthood*

Aileen Jarvis & Rowan Roffe

Mindful Parenting Made Simple

A FREE GIFT TO OUR READERS

As a way of saying thank you for your purchase, we're offering our readers special access to the ultimate mindful parenting checklist.

This checklist includes:

- 3 Mindful techniques to turn conflicts into closeness.
- 11 Powerful phrases for positive parenting that you can use TODAY.
- 15 Self-care strategies to help you own parenthood!

Visit this link: https://tinyurl.com/mindfulchecklist

Introduction

"Children are educated by what the grown-up is and not by his talk."

-by Carl Jung

Remember the time when the little one was coming into the world, gracing you with their presence while breaking nearly all the bones in your body? Or at least it felt like that. Remember the moment the doctor told you that you finally did it and that the worst was now over?

Fast forward three years and you are sitting on the kitchen floor scraping up Nutella or Vaseline that your toddler decided to paint the floor and walls with? And as soon as you take them to the bathroom to wash off the chocolate spread from their hair, you discover that your little one has draped the toilet seat and bathroom floors with toilet papers.

It is hard to process any sane thoughts at the moment. You are so angry that you are about to lose your sh*t. How in the world did the doctor so conveniently lied to your face telling you that the worst was over? And here you are, barely remembering the last time you take a break from cleaning the house or the last time you get a full 8 hours of sleep.

Sometimes you wish you believed other parents when they told you that YOU REALLY HAVE NO IDEA ABOUT HAVING KDIS UNTIL YOU HAVE KIDS! Children not only make you occasionally want to lose your sh*t, but you are also cleaning up after their sh*t, literally and figuratively. Seeing my children aspiring to be Pablo Picasso with Nutella and Vaseline, it's hard to remember the excitement I felt when they came to the world. I was ecstatic when they started crawling and even more thrilled when they took their first steps. But, had I anticipated what that meant, I would have probably appreciated some more time and perhaps more warnings of what children are capable of.

Dear readers, we are completely with you and quite frankly have been in the same boat as you. Parenting is hard. It feels like the whole world is conspiring against you. The man upstairs is watching from above, enjoying the back and forth running you do to get your child to eat or stay still while you are changing their leaking diaper. It feels like everyone else is sitting on a greener grass, having a glass of wine; meanwhile, you have been sent up onto the stage to perform a comedy gig - and you don't even know any jokes.

Being a parent is the world's toughest job. You are on call 24/7. You get no overtime, no PTO, and no definite job description. You are expected to deal with all source of problems, and losing your mind isn't one of the solutions.

So, what are we suggesting? Not to get frustrated when your kids misbehave right under your nose and keep doing it, just to get you all riled up? Or not to react when they are getting on your nerves demanding for some candy they don't remember the name of but saw it in the department store?

It is very easy to lose control of the situation and yourself in such frustrating moments and, like you, we have shared similar experiences at some point in our parenthood. Here's one thing we learned: those frustrating moments were the moments when staying calm and composed saves you your time and energy later in life.

When kids are young and naïve, they are all set to explore things on their own. They want to feel like kings and emperors who ruled the world and the people in it. Just with a motion of their hands, they got whatever they wanted. They want to feel the same control, freedom, and sovereignty. And we all know how the stories go. Whenever they felt challenged or scared, they brought out the big guns and the catapults… Kids; they may not have real weapons, but they do have the ability to make endless demand, cry, and cause a power struggle. Their tantrums and mischievousness may be a great story to share one day at a family gathering, but what about right now? How can we deal with their tantrums and mischievousness?

That is the big question that this book will answer. How can we, as parents, keep our sanity and be understanding? How can we be seen as empathic while maintaining boundaries and rules? How can we demand respect while being perceived as supportive and friendly and not dictatorial? How we can navigate through power struggles using practical behavioral adjustment strategies that don't come off as deliberate and pushy. How can we establish good habits for better emotional awareness and meaningful interactions?

This book will steer clear of any assertive tips but rather focus on mindfulness techniques for both parents and the kids, especially for first-time parents. We shall start this mindfulness journey with you, of course, and then move onto implementing similar techniques and methods on your kids. Together, we shall kick this off with a basic understanding of the daily struggles of parenthood, the frustrations and then introduce you to the many definitions of mindfulness, how to practice it and what crucial role it plays to improve the parent-child relationship.

This book isn't exactly scholarly, but it does hold some great insights and scientific research studies to help you understand the mental and cognitive processes better.

Why should you listen to what we have to say? What makes us the experts at parenting? Well, it is only fair to introduce us first so that, throughout the book, you know who we are and where we are coming from.

We are Aileen Jarvis & Rowan Roffe. We have come together to write this one of a kind book while both working as child development specialists. Our work takes us through the daily struggles that parents face as their children grow up. Inspired by the way in which we see children and their unique tendencies, and how it can affect a parent, we decided to write this parenting book that gives a voice to the frustration, so many of you parents feel. Parents of two and three children, respectively, we have incorporated both our own professional knowledge and personal experience in the writing of this book. We hope you will enjoy reading it through and find the answers you came looking for.

Chapter 1: What's Up, Chuck?

Parenthood is tough, and it usually takes the highest toll on the mothers, especially the ones who are mothers for the first time. They are figuring out the many changes in their bodies. Some may be dealing with postpartum depression without actually knowing that they have it while taking care of a newborn who is completely dependent on them for everything, forcing them to put their own needs second to that of their child's.

We get it. It's difficult. We have been through similar situations. Our stories echo the same battle and worries. We share your exhaustion and frustration… This is why Rowan and I are motivated to make parenthood easier for ourselves and for other parents to be. The feelings of worry, frustration, and anger during parenthood is normal, but these feelings shouldn't be normalized if we want to achieve a more rewarding parenting experience. Remember we are not managing inconvenience. We are raising a human being. Hence, we need to support each other and learn the habits that can make parenting a little easier. After all, most of us know there is more to come after the terrible twos.

Enter toddlerhood and adolescence.

The age where your lovingly-festooned house no longer looks like one. The age where everything turns chaotic with a lot of running involved but rarely having anything accomplished. The age where there are endless tantrums in a day and only more to come to the next. The age where quietness signals the calm before the storm and likely a sign of something sneaky going on behind your back. Maybe we are drawing a picture too dramatic. Still, even if nothing of the sort goes on into your house with a toddler, it is natural for you to feel parental frustration at some point. The annoyance can result from the kid not listening to you or obeying you. It can also result from misbehavior and ill-manners of your children, exacerbated by your struggles at work. Whatever the cause of your irritation is, it is an understandable response to the stress of parenthood even though it shouldn't be. Why do we say it shouldn't be? It is because the majority of the time, this frustration, even though difficult, is manageable. If you cannot control your response, your emotional outburst can result in an unintended effect, setting a less-than-stellar example for our kids.

Whenever we come across parents complaining to us about the use of foul language, the first thing we ask them is about the environment in their homes. Is it conducive to the kid's development? Does the way the parent discipline the child involve yelling and verbal and emotional mistreatment? Is the kid exposed to continuous fights between the adults in their life? Is one or both parents short-tempered? All of these questions allow us to better understand a child's experience and what's going on inside the mind of the kid. You see, kids are like sponges. They socialize by absorbing and imitating whatever they see and listen. They are quick to pick things up as their brain is constantly evolving. Therefore, it is crucial that children are exposed to the environment that is conducive to their development and that we parents exhibit the type of characters we want them to take after.

So how can you deal with the everyday frustrations that come with being a parent? How do you handle your emotions without causing a scene in front of your kids or punishing them when they might be mirroring you?

In this first chapter, we are going to be looking at this in detail and talk about how we can better understand the role we play in nurturing strong-willed, compassionate and emotionally intelligent kids.

To do so, let's first understand what frustration is or looks like so that we feel more prepared to deal with it later.

To end the first habit of frustration, you must start with noticing when you are frustrated and seeing if the cause is internal or external. This is the first key habit in adopting the first stage of mindful parenting

Introduce the habit of noticing when you are frustrated and analyzing the cause of it. Let's start there.

Understanding Frustration

Frustration, in psychology, is considered a natural but emotional response to opposition. It usually comes in the form of annoyance, anger, and disappointment. Frustration breeds from resistance to fulfilment of a person's goal or will and likelier to intensify when that goal or will is blocked or denied. In simpler terms, it is the uncontrollable rage that we feel when we find that something hasn't gone the way we expected it to. Parental frustration is similar. It is an expression of anger often accompanied by irritation and disappointment, resulting from unmet expectations.

There are two forms of frustration – internal and external. Internal frustration is the result of unmet personal goals, expectations, instinctual drives, needs, and desires. It can also be due to perceived deficiencies such as low self-esteem, lack of self-discipline, or other fears. Another cause of internal frustration can stem from internal conflict when one personal goal interferes with the other and causes one to feel conflicted and less sense of control. It can also lead to cognitive dissonance. If we were to see an example of internal frustration in our daily life, it looks something like this: you are having a difficult time at work. Responding to the workload, you spend more time at the office, which makes you miss precious time with your kid. However, because you are a parent, your child is the reason why you aren't able to give your work the time it deserves so that you can be a step closer to your professional goals. When you are at work, you think about your kid, and when you are with your kid, you think about work. You are bound to feel conflicted having to balance between work and kid and perhaps feel guilty that you sometimes have to choose work over your child.

On the other hands, external causes of frustration encompass conditions that aren't in our control and our need to control the uncontrollable leads us to feel like a failure. These causes may include physical roadblocks where other people and things get in the way of our goals. We may also feel frustrated due to our perception of wasting time. An example of frustration from external causes might look something like this: you are at the office and waiting for some report from another colleague to look at before you go home. You are already getting calls from your spouse because it is getting late, and you don't want to be stuck in the traffic for another hour before going home to your family. But that report is nowhere to be seen, and you have just been told that it will take another hour or so before the colleague finishes it. This situation is due to someone else's poor working ethic and is out of your control. You can't do anything to drastically change the outcome, so you feel frustrated as you have no control over the situation.

Parental Frustration and Its Primary Causes

Parental frustration usually arises from feelings of insecurity and uncertainty, which is a by-product of our inabilities to fulfil our or our kid's needs. When the needs are hindered by some external stimuli, frustration occurs. It can also originate when these needs are unsatisfied or constantly ignored. We feel agitated, angry, depressed, aggressive, or annoyed, and sometimes, we take it out in the worst form – violence. Violence isn't always physical. It can also be emotional, mental, or verbal.

Parental frustration is inevitable. When you are raising a kid, frustration is a given. They may be quick learners, but sometimes, they test your patience with making you repeat things over and over again. You want them to grow up to be the best version of themselves, and in doing so, you invest your time, energy, and money. Getting frustrated is normal. But how you deal with that frustration is the big question! Before we get to answering that, how about we take a look at some of the most frequent reasons that lead to parental frustrations? These reasons are the most common ones we come across when working with various families. We bet that the frustration you feel is also due to one of these reasons.

Undisciplined kid/kids

Kids who don't listen or purposely misbehave are the #1 reason for parents becoming frustrated. Not only is it embarrassing for the parents to deal with the misbehavior when it happens in crowded public spaces, but it also makes it harder for parents to apply positive discipline. Positive discipline is hard to accomplish when dealing with misbehavior because children respond more quickly to punishments, and positive disciplining requires more effort from parents. The literal meaning of the word discipline isn't punishment, but rather "to teach." This means that to discipline, we have to be mindful and use tools like communication and empathy to change a child's behavior rather than trying to stop their behavior by inflicting emotional or even physical pain with punishment. Sometimes, when we see other kids behaving well, it makes us even more frustrated because we know we are giving our all to foster our kids in the best way. We are always trying our best to meet their needs, listening to them, showing patience around them, and whatnot. Yet, they still choose to misbehave and throw tantrums. This makes parents wonder where are they falling short and what needs to be done.

Little Sense of Accomplishment

Raise your hands if you can relate to this: how many times have you felt that no matter how much you do for your kids, you always fall short at some point? There is always something lacking that makes you doubt your capabilities and feel like a failure. There are days when we feel like we didn't get anything done despite not having a minute to sit down and relax. This "little sense of accomplishment" can make us feel helpless when piling with an endless to-do list of laundry, grocery, etc.

We feel like we have spent the day catering to the needs of just your child, and even then your child still doesn't want to go to bed calmly at the end of the day. This can lead to frustration when you think about all the things you have to do and worry about pushing them for the next day, which by the way, already has another to-do list.

Poor Character in Kids

We want our kids to grow up as well-mannered and obedient individuals. Kids who lack a sound and disciplined foundation often become the cause of frustration among parents. After all, they are often viewed as a reflection of us and our parenting capabilities, and we want them to have a good character. We want them to have all those qualities we aspire to and want to see in ourselves as well as them. We want them to speak with integrity, not use foul language, have self-confidence, and depict good manners. When our kids lie, talk back to us, use a poor choice of words when angry or agitated, these things make us feel like we didn't do well enough.

Disorganization in the House

Nobody likes a disorganized and cluttered space. We have all been injured with the Lego blocks lying on the floor. We have also fallen prey to cleaning up after our kids are done playing because they chose sleeping over cleaning when you asked them to pick one of the two. Although you got them to sleep, you were left with the cleaning and arrangement of their million toys; and don't even get us started on how it just takes them a mere second to pull them all out from the toy basket when they can't find that one tiny army action figure. You get it, right?

No one likes to come home all tired and then feel they have to pick up after everybody and cook and clean. Parents aren't machines. We get tired too. But our children are young and naïve. They don't get the concept of being tired. All of this clutter, even though expected in a house with young children, can unexpectedly deepen our frustration.

Sibling Quarrels

Having one child can already be a handful; however, having more than one can create another source of frustration. While developing their sense of ownership, siblings can turn into rivals. One child will want what the other is playing with, and the other would want what the other sibling is playing with. They are never content with what they have and don't know how to share. Then, after trying to get their way and failing to get away with it, they come to you crying and complaining about who hit whom first and so on. This can take a toll on a parent who loves both the kids. Somehow, you manage to get them calmed down and learn to share, but that peace treaty only lasts a few minutes, and they are back at fighting over a new toy.

Having a Full Plate

One of the major mistakes that many parents make is being over-committed. We feel like we have to do it all, and we have no time for ourselves. And the fact that we can't do it all and have to compromise our personal needs is just outright frustrating.

Dealing With the Anger and Irritation

Now that we have established the many reasons that can cause parents to feel frustrated and lose their calm, the next step is to figure out how to deal with it. Being a parent constantly comes with new challenges. Some days, we feel like everything will be alright and that we will learn to live with it. But some days are downright tough and drain every last bit of our energy and patience.

Days when the little one falls sick and constantly cries or days when they keep on whining over every little thing from their dress to the food. During those days, it is easy to lose sight of the bigger picture, which is raising them to be a good person, instilling in them good habits and values. But as stated earlier, mindful parenting and positive disciplining start with you. Therefore, if you are feeling frustrated over something, the first step to addressing this emotion is to be aware of it. Examine the cause of this emotion and focus on how you can positively respond to it.

Importance of Recognizing the Negative Feelings

Anger and irritation are usually the first indications that something is not going right. However, before letting them overwhelm us and make us lose our minds, we need to understand where it is stemming from. Generally, is this frustration due to some internal or external causes? What behavior from your child triggers it? Is it some repeated action like not eating their vegetables or resisting a bath?

You need to recognize those feelings of negativity and address them. The best way to do so is to accept them as they come. Accept that you are feeling angry and don't try to cover it up with some other emotion. Find an outlet for this emotion if you must. Secondly, please don't blame yourself or feel ashamed for feeling the negative emotion. It is okay to feel a little mad and agitated over how your kid makes you feel. What is not okay is acting negatively in response to these emotions. The best way to deal with frustration, especially the one with an external source is to recognize the wisdom of the Serenity Prayer—"God grant me the serenity to accept the things I cannot change; courage to change the things I can; and wisdom to know the difference."

We come across many parents who are extremely overwhelmed because they find their experience as parents different from their expectation. They keep bottling up their emotions, which drive them to a breaking point. Every emotion, be it negative or positive, needs addressing and acknowledgement. Acknowledging our emotions is necessary for emotional acceptance.

Many mothers, for instance, complain of unsupportive partners. Feeling unsupported and lack of teamwork creates negative feelings, which can be amplified when children misbehave. Sometimes children are just being children, and we adults lack the emotional intelligence to address our issues that we sometimes unconsciously projected them onto the kids. Hence, if at any time you feel frustrated and don't know how to react, here are a few things you can do to help yourself feel better and in a calmer state of mind.

One of the recommendations we make for parents when they feel that they are losing control of their emotions is to distance themselves from the thing that is triggering the anger or irritation. This means if your work, partner, or your kid is getting on your nerves and you sense an outburst of negative emotions ready to take over, temporarily remove yourself from that space so that you give yourself some room to breathe. Excuse yourself to avoid any conflicting situations, which can only make matters worse. Go into another room and let the emotions run through you or until the wave of emotions subsided. Don't go back into the situation unless you are more clam and have accepted the negative emotion. Take at least ten deep breath until your heartbeat slows down, and you feel more in control over your emotions.

If you have little to no control over the trigger, and there isn't much you can do, the best way to deal with the overwhelming feeling is either to talk to someone. Talking through your emotions with a close friend can be beneficial. You can also write them down in a journal. The idea is to not let your emotions get all bottled up because they are going to manifest themselves in some ways, and the way they manifest themselves might be in the manner you prefer. Once we have talked through our emotions or expressed them on a piece of paper, we will start to feel calm again. Most of the time, when we are overwhelmed, the best way to handle it is to get these feelings out of our systems. Talking through our feeling and writing them down is a great opportunity to reflect on the situation and start to see things more clearly. The biggest disadvantage of bottling up our negative feelings is that this can cloud our judgment and affect our sanity. We need to learn to express our emotions constructively so that our emotions don't emerge in a way that negatively impacts the people we care about.

Another effective but quite random advice we recommend to parent is to take the approach Fred Rogers adopt (for completely different reasons) in the popular TV show *Mister Rogers' Neighborhood*. Interestingly, changing clothes can also be a mood changer as it allows our mind to think about something other than the negative emotion. The idea is to get busy elsewhere so that one stops thinking about the frustration and let go of it. This is referred to as making a mental and physical shift from a negative emotion to a positive one. A simple act such as changing clothes can help let go of the emotions one feels too strongly. Once you are able to remove yourself from the situation temporarily, you will be able to see the situation more clearly, figure out why you felt so out of control, and learn to deal with it more positively next time.

Why Does Modern-day Parenting Look So Hard?

Since this question comes up quite often when we coach parents, it is only fair that we make a comparison between our generation and that of our parents. Think about it; they seemed to have done it so easily. They fed, cleaned, and looked after us. They had time to attend kiddie parties, wedding events, and other social parties without thinking a dozen times who will watch the kids and whether we should go at all or not. Of course, we are busier than our parents, but that only means more stress and frustration for us. With the amount of time we have with our kids, we have to teach them good manners, instil in them good habits, discipline them, and make them grow into responsible individuals.

We have worked with more mothers than you can imagine, and every time we are amazed at how smart, intellectual, well-resourced, and educated parents of today are. The parenting problems we faced today are so different from the issues faced by our parents decades ago. Issues like cyberbullying, data privacy, screen time, etc. are all the problems that emerge and become more prevalent in the last decade. The level of frustration many parents of today feel when dealing with these issues is astounding.

Frustration seems to be the threads that weave the modern-day parents together. But it isn't just frustration that is the problem. It is also self-doubt, worries, anxiety, and judgmental looks that we sometimes get from our parents and grandparents who might think we are doing a poor job of parenting. Sometimes we feel ashamed of the messiness and how chaotic our life is. Other times we feel like we don't have what it takes to keep up with others and thus feel guilty, which makes us even more frustrated.

So why do we feel this defeated, burned out, and inadequate all the time even though we are better resourced than any generation of mothers?

Let's take a look at the differences in modern-day parenting and old-style parenting and understand why it is harder to raise good kids today than it has ever been. (Just to be clear, this is a gross generalization of the modern and traditional parenting.)

Nowadays, our expectations as parents have risen. The bar for what is considered "good parents" are set higher. And the worst part: support has dropped. We have come a long way from an era where shaming, beating, scaring, and threatening children was considered a norm. Now, although it's a good thing in general that we are more aware of the life-long impact of such old practices, the shift in the child-rearing models has eliminated many important players that helped with raising a child. Think grandmas, aunts, cousins, and neighbours. In the old-time, many families used to have joint family systems that offered comfort and support. There were whole tribes taking care of children, supportive neighbourhoods where kids played outside in the sun all day, and family members who were always happy to take in the kids when we wanted some time of our own. Now, we have to worry about hiring someone professional, relying on their expertise, paying them. If that isn't an option, we have to pick and drop them at the daycare so that they can be looked after while we are at work.

Being a parent, especially a mother, is an all-consuming job. We feel constantly bombarded with what ideal parenting should look like and fear being judged or shamed for the way we parent. There is never-ending pressure of looking and acting a certain way, thanks to all the advertising and celebrity images that we see every day. They seem to have it all figured out and look flawless like they are able to sleep 8 hours a day and have time to do their hair and makeup. What many fail to remember is that we only see the best part of people on social media. Celebrities often have a full-time helper. We, on the other hand, are the ones cleaning their poop, changing their diapers, spending the whole day looking after them. Expecting our parenthood to be as effortless as what we see on social media is not realistic.

Another reason for the added pressure is that women of today aren't just expected to become full-time moms. We are also expected to build our careers simultaneously and be exceptional at work and at home. Then, we are also expected to look good, appearance-wise, not show any signs of ageing, discomfort, or pain even when the high heels are killing us, and the earrings are just too heavy. And once we are done showing off to the world how great we look and feel, we have to come home to our kids and worry about their cleaning, eating, food sensitivities, internet safety, sustainability, manners, school affairs, and their emotional and physical wellbeing. It seems like too much, doesn't it?

The abundance of knowledge and wisdom we receive from the digital world urges us to do more with that knowledge. However, conflicting ideas, ever-changing dynamics, and false bits of advice linked to promotional products and services make it harder for us discern which advice is essential and applies to us.

We are sleeping less, suffering from low energy levels, and have too much to worry about at once. The worst thing about parenting is that you never get any cheat days. Once a parent, always a parent! This role becomes your whole life, and that starts to get you.

We feel exhausted because we have to fill in so many roles at once. We have to be our kid's best pal, their playmate, mentor, teacher, nutritionist, maid, and their mother. Women, in particular, battle with exhaustion as they are wired to care about the needs of others and often put those needs above our own.

Moreover, we are also up against the biggest marketing giants. They are feeding our kids with senseless, gender-biased, addictive messages. They are normalizing the drinking of Coke, eating a Big Mac for lunch, heading to Hardy's for some milkshakes leaving us parents to deal with the corresponding urges and tantrums. Not to mention the excessive screen time and what it is doing to our kid's minds, eyesight and body is an issue big enough to write another book about. Imagine having to protect a little one from all that is out there for them and constantly feeling like you're losing the battle.

The challenges that come with modern parenting can be an exhaustive list; however, the goal of mindful parenting is for us to be present and aware of our external and internal situations so that we can respond thoughtfully to our children's behaviors and actions in a way that nurtures the relationship.

Chapter 2: Mindfulness Exposed

Have you ever had a day where you were already late to work, and as you walked towards the door, you felt something grab you by the feet? Like two little hands, clinging onto your skirt or pants, looking up to you with their puppy-dog eyes? As much as you would want to capture that moment in your memory forever, you know that if you don't make it past the door this very minute, you are going to be awfully late and miss the presentation you have been tirelessly working on for weeks.

The first thought that crosses your mind is, "Oh God, not today" because you are fully aware of what follows after the little one has gotten your attention and moved your heart with that gesture. Parenting can be extremely hard when kids keep testing your patience and challenging your ways. When Rowan and I started our career as a child development specialist, we were naïve back then. Even though we had studied child psychology in-depth and dealt with the pressures of it firsthand, we still lacked that balance we hoped to create. You know that level of calm and peace in the house where there is a strong parent-child relationship, and the kids don't misbehave. We always wanted that kind of peace in our house too. But with more than one kid in the house, that seemed like an impossible dream.

Like many other parents, we tried every trick in many parenting books to become better parents and establish an amazing relationship with our children. Still, nothing seemed to provide us with the result we wanted. Our children were immuned to the way we disciplined them. Their compliance was short-lived, and disobedience continued. They hated us when we tried to discipline them, and it was costing our relationship. That was the time when there was this crazy hype about mindfulness. Everyone was talking about it with enthusiasm. Articles were being written, papers being published, research being done. It seemed to be the next big thing that the world had waited for.

Reading about it and discussing its many benefits with ourselves, we wondered if we could try to apply some of the mindfulness practice at home with our kid. Initially, we were skeptical that something so vague would ever work, but the minute we started, we noticed little changes in the behavior of our kids; we knew that we were a step closer to the dream home environment we had wanted.

The kids started to become more expressive about their demands and needs, showed patience when told to wait, and began confiding with us the things that bothered them. Conversations about anything and everything become a common thing in the house, and together, as a unit, we all worked to meet each other's expectations. This might seem like quite a poetic explanation of what worked for us but, to tell you the truth, it was no light-bulb moment. We learned through trial and error, modified things our way, and actually made an effort to change the things we wanted to change.

Since we were new to the terminology, and there was little information about mindful parenting, we had to make some major changes in our attitudes and behaviors as well. Since we knew that implementing mindfulness practices in parenting meant we had to first walk the talk, learn to wear our kid's shoes and see the world from their eyes, it was extremely hard not to lose our tempers when dealing with them and then address every tantrum differently. This might seem quite a lot to take in for now, but by the time you are done reading this book, we are hopeful that you will feel comfortable practicing and honing these techniques.

In this chapter, let's first go through the basics of mindfulness, mindful parenting, and practices every new mindful parent can use to keep negative emotions in control. Once we have these sorted out, we'll move on to some role-playing and see how the kids view their parents and what goes in their minds. Yes, things are going to get super exciting moving forward.

What Is All the Hype About Mindfulness?

The best way to describe mindfulness is this: Imagine you are driving around the city, perhaps on a trip all by yourself. You arrive at the destination, and the people there ask you how the drive was. It is then that it clicks that you hardly remember anything about it. You remember passing through some fields, some big advertising boards, but not the route or specific turns you took. The whole drive was a blur.

Another example can be watching TV while eating dinner simultaneously. Some people have a hard time recalling what they had for dinner last night because they were operating on autopilot. Let me be clear, there is nothing wrong with enjoying food while watching our favorite TV shows; however, in a culture where productivity is valued, multitasking can be a slippery slope that leads to mindlessness—a state where one seems to lose track of time completely and is rarely able to recall anything meaningful regarding the occurrence. It is a state of being in the autopilot mode where our body repeats actions that we are used to performing without the brain ever registering them. Did you know that humans are in an "autopilot" mode 47% of the time (Killingsworth & Gilbert, 2010)?

How do we ever let our mind wander this way? It's like being in a dreamlike state without actually falling asleep. This is very similar to being drunk as the brain isn't capable of actively making wise decisions. Imagine you hit someone crossing the street while driving because you weren't paying attention to the new crosswalk in your neighborhood. This sounds scary, doesn't it? But, being on autopilot is human nature. In some ways, it helps the brain saves energy and helps us get through our everyday life. However, at times this mindlessness can work against us and our intentions.

For example, we sometimes fail to notice the signals our body gives us to rest or that there is an early symptom of more serious illnesses. Maybe our back is aching, and because it doesn't interfere with our daily activities, we ignore it and carry on with our lives until it becomes a more serious issue.

Mindlessness isn't just harmful to us, but can also later impact the lives of people around us. Being in an autopilot state helps prevent our brain from becoming overload. However, it may come at an emotional cost when it slips into the areas of our lives that require more forethought. When we sleepwalk into our choices, this increases the likelihood of us making poor choices causing us to be more stressed and anxious. The same research mentioned previously, for instance, also suggests that the more we let our minds wander, the less happy we are as we fail to notice the beauty of things around us.

Now imagine a state completely opposite of mindlessness. This is what we call mindfulness. It is coming out of the autopilot mode and taking control. Mindfulness is becoming aware of the present, aware of what we are doing and what we are not doing. It is the ability to be fully human so that we don't get swept away by our emotions. We all possess the quality to become mindful. We are born with it; however, kids have an easier time to be mindful. See how babies look at you with their eyes wide open even when they do not understand a word you are saying? Notice how they smile back at you when you grin at them? These are all the ways they are being mindful of their presence with yours. Sadly, due to the Western culture of productivity and multitasking, many children will lose their natural tendency to be present over time, unless we nurture this mindfulness in them.

Since we already possess mindfulness since birth, all we need to do is cultivate it using simple strategies so that we can appreciate the "now" and begin to accept things without judgment. These basic strategies include breathing techniques, sitting quietly with our self-reflective thoughts, enjoying peaceful walks, and mindful meditation. There are many benefits associated with these simple techniques, the majority of them leading to a complete sense of awareness which we want to foster in our kids.

Being fully present help to us to be emotionally grounded, allow us to shift from negative thinking to a more positive one, and enable us to make choices that best reflect our interests. It also helps us to be more aware, reduces stress, and enables us to approach things with more compassion, kindness, and less judgment.

Since you are role models for your kids, it is only fair that we start with you.

Mindfulness and Parenting: What's the Connection?

Paying attention has become so difficult these days. With the advent of phones and increased screen time in the form of media channels like Netflix, Amazon Prime, Disney, and Hulu, we are always looking for a more meaningful time. This screen usage upsurge has also affected our focus as we try to do more things but less focus to do them. So, we keep on multitasking, hoping to have a foot in everything and not miss out.

Even when we do try to fully engage in one thing, our mind is constantly wandering elsewhere, worrying about something entirely different. We are always geared at thinking about the next thing and how we are going to do that. In short, we have stopped living in the moment, or appreciate the here and now. When we're not mindful, a majority of our time is spent thinking about the past or the future—creating unnecessary emotional focus toward the things or events we have no control over. How many times have we stopped to wonder about the impact of our own mindlessness on our little ones? Do they deserve such a distracted parent?

Mindful parenting focuses on giving our kids the best thing in the world: our undivided attention and time. It is our presence, our acceptance, and an opportunity to create meaningful, strong, and long-lasting relationships that they want. And we all know how good it feels to be fully immersed into something that we love doing. We feel so alive and so empowered. We feel valued and on cloud nine. Imagine our kids feeling the same way. Imagine our children looking up to us with compassion in their eyes because they feel looked after, safe, and cared for. This is truly the best gift we can ever give them.

Becoming mindful is easier when there is less frustration, anger, or judgment involved. As stated before, these things cloud our thinking, and we lose the chance to build a connection with our kids. Every time we meet parents who complain of disobedience, we ask them how they react to situations where the child break the rules or does something that embarrassed them. Most of the parents respond with answers like giving their children cold stares, yelling, scolding, and even at times, hitting. As you may know, all these actions – the one thing we have to control, are not part of positive parenting, and they are classic indicators of frustration and anger.

We often tell parents that instead of losing their temper, they should view it as an opportunity to make things right in a calm and composed manner. That is when the kids need the acceptance of who they are from their parents. They want to be assured that, even though they messed up, their parents still love them. So grab that opportunity with both hands and make the most of it. It doesn't mean that you look over your child's mistake and misbehavior, but rather you sit them down and let them know that although they did something wrong, you aren't mad. Make it a point that the behavior they depicted is not acceptable and that you would very much appreciate it if they didn't repeat it. Tell them what your expectations are of them and ask if they would like to say something as well. The idea is to not let them feel like they are being schooled or lectured but rather being talked to with concern.

We know for a fact that almost three-fourth of parents see parenting as the biggest challenge they ever had to face, but if you do as stated above, you will soon realize that disciplining isn't as hard as it sounds. All we need is to find the right tools and use the right strategies to raise a sensible, emotionally intelligent, and well-mannered child.

If you continue to see parenting as a difficult chore, which, frankly it can be, you will keep finding it hard at every step of the way. You will feel stressed when you have to change diapers, feed your kids, and worry about what's best for them – all the while, doubting your own choices and judging your own parenting capabilities. What if we tell you that perfection is not the goal of being a better parent and that it is time we let go of the idea of "being perfect," altogether? There is no such thing as perfect parenting, as every parent faces different and unique challenges with their kids. No two kids are alike, which sadly, makes parenting a bit harder. What might have worked with your elder one might not work with your younger one.

However, what DOES work, regardless of which children it is, is mindful parenting. It all begins with accepting the things you can't control. You can't control your child's preferences and personality. Do not compare them with their siblings and peers. The fact that your child is different from their siblings and peers does not mean that you are doing something wrong. When we begin to look at mindful parenting as the ability to become fully present and pay attention to our kids with compassion, kindness, and respect, we begin to love them even more naturally because we see them for their uniqueness, for who they are and not who we wish them to be.

Practicing Mindful Parenting: A Guide for Beginners

Keep in mind that while we suggest mindful parenting, it isn't synonymous with becoming the perfect parents to your kids. There will be times when you will fail and rethink the advice you took from this book. Learning to be mindful and accepting the situation at hands is s a learning process. You can expect it to be hard, but not impossible. You are going to get the hang of it eventually and figure out the techniques that best work for you and your kid/kids.

Before we get to this insider's guide, we must tell you that, as beginners, it is going to take some patience on your part and a whole lot of practice. Some days will be good and the others not so much. You may give in to your emotions some days and some days learn to control them. But keep in mind that every step of the way, you will be left with two choices – either to react spontaneously or to pause, reflect, then respond.

Taking a moment to contemplate before responding is the essence of becoming a mindful parent. You pay attention to what's happening in the present and not get carried away by your emotions. Throughout the process of becoming mindful, you will learn to let go of any shame and guilt about the actions of your past and focus on dealing with the ones you feel presently. You simply learn to accept things as they happen rather than doing anything about it or attempting to change or ignore them. But that doesn't mean you can't or won't get angry. You will still sense the negative feelings brewing up inside you like a fresh pot of coffee; however, you will stop responding to them mindlessly.

Below are some of the basic steps you need to keep a note of when adopting mindful parenting.

Give Your Child Your Full Attention

Sometimes, all one needs is an ear to tell things to. Be that person for your child. You must be wondering, isn't that all that we do? But amidst all the things, this is the one thing we aren't doing. We may think we are, but we are prone to multitasking with an attention span of fewer than eight seconds. Even when we do sit down to hear their thoughts, imaginations, and ideas, we fail to listen to what they are truly trying to tell us.

Listening is an essential step to becoming a mindful parent. This is the first habit you need to adopt. Try to understand what they mean when they are telling things. They may not always use the best choice of words or use no words at all, but that is when we need to focus on their body language and actions to understand what they are trying to say. For example, a toddler crying in a stroller or seeming uneasy means that they may want to get out of it. Or, maybe they're hungry, or just tired. Their crying and uneasiness are what you need to interpret and act upon.

When you begin to listen and pay attention, you learn how to respond better.

Accept Who They Are (Even When They Annoy You)

Judging someone based on their actions, behavior, or mood is the easiest thing to do in the world. Sometimes, we do the same with our kids and in a rather harsh manner. Some days they will be hard to handle. Those are the days when you have to stay patient and not give in to your negative feelings. After all, ask yourself this: does punishment by scolding, for example, really work? Generally, it gets your children attention; however, long term, would scolding foster a good relationship between you and your child? If your answer is no, then we have to accept the fact that sometimes your child's behaviour will deviate from your expectation and your responsibility is to accept and find the cause of their behavior.

If they are being hard, annoying or needy, don't tell them to act older than their age and "get it together before dad comes home." Don't scare them into changing who they are. Some kids just need an extra dose of love and care. Offer them that and notice how the acting out will cease after some time. Acceptance of their feelings and letting them know that you understand what they are going through is an instant trust-builder. As a mindful parent, you need to be their rock and support them.

Feel What They Are Feeling

This means putting yourself in their shoes sometimes and viewing the world how they are viewing it. If they don't want to get into the bath and cry their eyes out, imagine how they are feeling. Ask yourself, why would they not want to take a bath? Are they scared? If they cry over not finding their favorite blanket before bedtime, imagine what they must be going through. What is your usual reaction when you can't find something important to you? You feel a mixture of anger, frustration, and tears. They are feeling the same. They just don't know how to handle it appropriately. Again, when you try to understand their point of view, your response to any given situation changes, and you become more compassionate and caring.

Dealing With Frustrations and Anger Using Mindfulness

You often find yourself in the fight or flight mode throughout the day. This can make you look at your kid as the enemy because you are too swept with anger to think things through and deal with the problem they are facing. Sometimes, the anger gets to the point that some parents consider physical punishment if the situation continues. Our stress causes our muscles to go all tense, breathing to quicken and our pulse to race. It becomes almost impossible to stay in control as the

Hulk in all of us is ready to rip off its clothes and throw its wrath upon the enemy.

But, take a breath. Even though you may get angry - very angry - with your child, there's no reason to act on that anger, be it with words or with other actions that exert your power over your child. Even when yelling at your child seems like a solution for anger relief, it really isn't. As their parent, you are foremost their guardian. Your role is to keep them safe from all the things they are scared of and not become another person or thing that your child is afraid of.

This leads to the second rule to becoming a mindful parent, and that is to not react in a state of anger. No sane decisions are made when one is angry. The only thing that follows when reacting in anger is immense regret, which is something we don't want you to go through. So instead of giving in to the urge of "teaching" your kid a lesson then and there, opt to discipline them at a later time when you are at a higher mental state. Your child isn't going anywhere. You can always sit them down whenever you want and instil some wisdom in them. You might be wondering, "easier said than done," and that's true. It will take practice. But trust us on this. To make it easier for you, we are listing some of the best mindfulness practices to adopt when you feel frustrated or angry about your child.

Address the Elephant in the Room

The first exercise involves acknowledgement. Everything has to start from you accepting the negative feelings as they come instead of running from them. Give yourself a verbal reason as to why you are feeling the way you are and what is causing it. If it is your kid that is making you angry, say this to yourself, "I am angry because he/she did [action]."

Next, analyze those emotions. Find out where they are coming from and are they truly related to the present situation or just some venting over something else? Here, you must identify if the emotions are in line with what is happening and whether this is how you should be reacting or not. This calls for an analysis of how major or minor the situation is. For instance, refusing to take a bath shouldn't get you all riled up and yell at your toddler. Why? Because this isn't the first time they are refusing to bathe, and you also know it isn't going to be the last either.

So, this is really just a minor issue and something you deal with daily. It shouldn't rile you up to the extent that results in shouting. If it does, then there is something else that is concurrently bothering you, and perhaps you bottled it up earlier. This means your anger is entirely about something else. This refusal, however, has tipped the glass over that was filled with anger to the brim. Now, unless you resolve that primary issue and acknowledge it, you aren't going to find a resolution to your emotional turmoil, and neither will your child understand why you're so upset.

Finally, we want you to think things through, which means we want you to inspect your reactions before they happen. The best way to do so is to imagine the situation as if it were reversed. Imagine you were the one being shouted at. Were you expecting such an overwhelming response? How did it make you feel? When you know how the other person feels, and how you would have felt had you been in their position, you begin to think twice before addressing your anger.

The STOP Discipline

This is a rather interesting way to deal with frustration and anger. The STOP discipline refers to four different things, with each playing a critical role in helping you react to situations mindfully. Here's how you can use it to your benefit.

S: The S stands for "stop". The first step is to cease and take a pause. It entails coming to terms with what is happening and how it is affecting you. This is only possible when you detach yourself from the situation and begin to analyze your emotions.

T: The T stands for "taking a deep breath" and later exhaling slowly. Repeat this at least seven times. More oxygen in your system helps calm your racing heart – something you will need in order to focus better.

O: The O stands for "observing your reactions and emotions" once you begin breathing in and out. You should feel less tense and feel calmness spreading through your mind, body, and spirit.

P: Finally, the P stands for "proceed," which means you can respond, now that you are more aware of yourself and your emotions. Chances are, you will feel less frustrated and respond with logic instead of anger.

Ignite the Coal

This is another great practice for when you feel out of control and ready to unleash your wrath upon your little ones or anyone in general. The COAL technique includes:

Curiosity

Openness

Acceptance

Love

All of which are steps to help resolve any issue in a calm manner. It starts with you taking a few deep breaths and detaching yourself from the situation. You can either leave the room, request a few minutes of peace or simply sit down and bring your child in a hug.

Curiosity: Starting with the first step, you need to be curious in figuring out what is making you this mad. Is it just the kid, or are there other things bothering your peace of mind too?

Openness: Next, you need to try to strike a conversation with your kid in a way that doesn't invoke more crying or whining. Ask them what they need but tell them that for you to understand them better they need to pause their cry and talk to you about it. This works best with children who have some basic verbal skills. During this openness stage, you need to be open to your children's needs and pay attention without judgment. Once you are able to connect with your child and get their attention, notice the changes in their behavior and expressions. Do they stop crying? What is the tone of their voice?

Acceptance: Acknowledge and accept that little initiation with warmth and support to let them know that you understand what they need and why they need it. This is the part where you respond to them with empathy.

Love: Finally, let them know that they are loved irrespective of what they did wrong.

Notice the drastic change in their attitude when it dawns on them that their parents understand their concerns and pay attention to them. That is the kind of bond you need to nurture from an early stage so that the highest level of trust is established between the parent and the child. If this works, which most of the time it will, you will never have to worry about your child hiding stuff from you or going behind your back with something mischievous. They will begin to acknowledge your feelings too, as they know that you are forgiving and willing to listen. So they will begin to ask for things rather than crying for them. That should be the goal of every mindful activity.

Take a Nap

Sounds like a great plan, but this isn't the nap we are talking about here. Here, NAP refers to noticing, allowing, and passing on.

Let's break it down using an example. Picture this: your kid has the flu and is more emotionally sensitive than usual.

Every little thing is upsetting him. They are crying over what they want to eat instead of what you made for them, not willing to change into new clothes and wanting to stay in their pajamas all day, even when they need to be laundered.

This has been going on for two days now, and you are on the verge of losing patience with them. You have tried everything to keep them calmed and help them feel as comfortable as possible while being sick, but they are refusing to take their meds and are crying non-stop. As much as your heart hurts looking at them, you just want to escape into another parallel universe because you can't take it anymore. They are pushing the limit of your patience, and you know it!

Notice: A mindful way of dealing with this situation starts with noticing the painful sensations your body experiences along with the kind of thoughts crossing your mind. They may not be all positive and uplifting, but noticing them is the first step to making things better.

Allow: Next, you have to allow these emotions and accept them without changing them. Then, you wait for them to pass on, which is the third step of this exercise.

Pass on: Allowing negative emotions to pass through your system is bidding them goodbye for good and releasing yourself from them. Remember nothing lasts forever, even negative emotions.

This acceptance practice prepares us to deal with negative feelings and emotions without running away from them. With practice, you will soon become a master of taking a NAP even in the most difficult situation.

Breathe in, Breathe Out

This is probably the oldest trick in the book, and often also the first one that comes to our minds when we hear the word mindfulness. But what we fail to understand is the importance it holds in our daily lives. It isn't something just useful when trying out some yoga poses. It is ideal in all those situations where we sense a loss of patience and frustration settling in. It is especially excellent when dealing with everyday tantrums; practicing mindful breathing daily and as many times as possible will facilitate us in handling stressful situations better.

We all are familiar with the basic mindful breathing. We start by closing our eyes and taking a deep breath until our stomach starts to ache a little. Then, we release and exhale out the trapped air slowly, and repeat the same until we feel calmness seeping inside us. This not only gives our organs an extra bout of air but also halts the production and release of chemicals like cortisol in the body, which triggers stress and anxiety. The more stress we feel, the less capable we are of controlling our emotions. And when we give in to negative emotions, they further promote the negativity. Think about it, when a kid receives a sound yelling or lecture, do they stop crying, or do they increase it a pitch further?

Blow Off Steam

Blowing off steam refers to diverting and channelling your anger to things or activities other than the thing or person that causes the anger. These activities could be going to the gym, a dance party, or singing at the top of your lung. Not many people support this form of releasing frustration as it doesn't solve the root of the problem; however, when it comes to parenting, especially with younger kids, who we want to see flourish with good habits and qualities, it can be a lifesaver. You begin by detaching yourself from the situation that is causing anger, and instead, turn to something else to let it all out. This technique works similarly to when your boxing trainer tells you to picture someone or something you hate and channel your energy to the punching bag. The idea is to not keep anything bottled up as it only complicates things further and relieves our systems of any negative emotions and feelings. However, blowing off steam doesn't damage some other thing or hurt someone else; it simply means looking for a healthy outlet for your anger and aggression.

Physical activity, like boxing, is a great cardiorespiratory workout and also a stress reducer. It causes the brain to release endorphins, the neurotransmitter that generates the sense of well-being, a.k.a. the feel-good chemical. Body movement during physical activities also helps to relieve muscle tension that accumulates from stress. Other suggestions for healthy ways to blow off steam are going for a run, calling a friend to vent about the situation, and journaling. As long as you're being responsible and mature about how you channel your negative emotion, activities like these can be very helpful. If your kids are old enough to understand, you can even tell them what you're doing: "I (Mommy/Daddy) am frustrated at the moment. I am boxing to blow off some steam so that I don't do or say something that might accidentally hurt other's feelings. Please give me fifteen minutes (or however long you need)."

Practice Self-Compassion

Treat yourself and your kids with compassion. Part of becoming more mindful begins with self-compassion, where you learn to let go of the mistakes you make as a parent and learn to love yourself. You have to stop comparing yourself with other parents and the methods they use. Not everything applies directly to you, so you have to stop thinking that you are a bad parent when your kids act out or misbehave. We are the first ones to criticize ourselves. We keep reminding ourselves that we aren't doing enough and that frustrations keep on building inside us until one day, we finally vent it out on either our partners or kids. Self-compassion, of course, isn't something that comes naturally for some of us who are perfectionists, but with practice, we can learn to have more compassion for ourselves. One technique is to use visualization. Imagine the traits or characteristics you would like to develop to be a better parent while accepting yourself and your kids where you currently are.

Here's how to practice it at home.

Start with finding yourself a comfortable and distraction-free space to sit in. Take a deep breath and let it out slowly. You can choose to keep your eyes open or closed, whichever way you prefer. Next, name the emotion you are feeling. Say it yourself out loud while continuing to take deep breaths and exhaling. Notice how your body reacts when you name the emotion. Does it tense up, loosen, or go into an uncomfortable stance? After that comes the acceptance part. Place both your hands on your heart and imagine you are holding it in between the palms of your hands. Gently caress it and visualize that you are filling your heart with love and kindness. For a more visual representation, view kindness as a bright light entering your heart and lighting up everything in the surroundings too. Continue taking deep breaths, and until you feel your body loosening up, continue visualizing that.

Once you are positive that the emotion you felt is now replaced with kindness in your heart, let your hands go back into their original position, stand up, and resume your normal daily activity. We recommend that you repeat this visualization every day so that you are kinder and more compassionate to yourself. Parenting is hard enough. You don't need to make it harder by being unkind to yourself.

Respond Instead of React

We briefly introduced you to the idea of this earlier because this is one of the most remarkable things you need to work upon to improve your relationship with your child and instil in them some ideal habits. This comes recommended by Job, Kabat-Zinn and Myla, co-authors of the book, Everyday Blessings, The Inner Work of Mindful Parenting. Throughout the book, the authors have distinguished between the two states of mind - reacting and responding. To a beginner, these may seem synonymous at first glance, but they are far from being equal.

Reacting is the state of being mindless. It usually refers to an immediate and rather irrational response resulting from one's emotions driven by attachments and expectations. We all set certain hopes and expectations with our kids, and when they fail to live up to them, we become angry and frustrated. Reacting without thinking seems like the right thing to do as we believe we have given them all the resources they need to act a certain way. Take, for instance, a kid who fails a class, and the father's first reaction is to punish their child by yelling and grounding the kid. Since the father thinks he had provided the kid with all the resources they needed to pass the class and still failed to live up to the set expectations, he thinks that his punishment is justified. However, let examine this for a minute. How are yelling and grounding beneficial to the child's educational development? Would it change the letter on the report card?

Responding, in comparison to reacting, is an act of mindfulness. It is where the individual thinks before reacting mindlessly or giving in to their first knee-jerk reaction. It involves scrutiny but free of judgment. You take some time before responding and think of the reasons why something happened and what calls for a suitable response. If we consider the example from above, the father, instead of yelling and grounding the child would think about what could have led the kid to fail, form an appropriate response that doesn't involve demotivation and then try to initiate a conversation once the response has been delivered empathetically and proactively. In this case, the child will be more willing to open up and talk about why they think they might have failed in the first place. It may be because the class was not a subject of the child's interest, or the child is being bullied at school. In both cases, the child will need the support of parents to figure out their passion or learn how to deal with peer conflicts.

Now that you have seen both reacting and responding in practice, which seems to be more promising? Which one do you think your child would prefer if they were in a similar situation? Which method do you think will nurture a mutually respectful relationship between you and your child?

Becoming Empathetic Towards Kids

This brings us to the importance of being empathetic towards children. We have become so used to spontaneously reacting that we have forgotten how to respond. Of all the things kids need the most, acceptance, care, and interest take the top three places on the stands. It is what they crave the most. They want to be accepted for who they are, even when they misbehave and act out of order. Especially then. It is like they are testing their parents to see if their love is conditional or not. Second, they need to know that they can come up to you with any concern and worry and they will be looked after. Think of caring as a blend of love and safety that every child wants to have. Lastly, they want to see their parents interested in and committed to them. They want to know if their parents are good listeners, show concern about their feelings, and value their opinions or not, no matter how stupid and naïve they are.

Give any child these three things, and they will turn out to be well-raised, decent, and mindful kids.

Now picture this being put into practice. Your kid has trouble getting dressed and getting down for breakfast on time. This has been happening for over a week now, and you are done shouting and yelling, "Breakfast is ready! Come down now, or you will miss your school bus." You want them to show some maturity and get ready on time for once. Every day, little by little, your frustration and anger are building g up, and today feels like the day when it will all come out if they don't "get down this minute." You tell them that if they don't come down this minute, you will confiscate all their toys as they are making you late for work too.

This is a very normal reaction, right? Many of us have been in a similar situation at some point in our lives too. But what you don't see is that reacting in such a manner is only relieving you of your frustration, but not getting their issues resolved. Your child still seems to have problems managing time, and your venting out isn't going to help. You are only releasing yourself of the negativity without taking into account what is happening with your kid. They are also struggling with something, i.e., getting ready, and would maybe prefer some help over yelling.

If, in this scenario, you choose to show empathy instead, it will change the whole dynamic of the current situation. How so? Showing empathy means you not only acknowledge your feelings but are also concerned about the feelings of your child. You take a moment to understand what your child is feeling. Instead of further causing them trouble and worry, you help take some of it off their shoulders by being kind and empathetic. Ask your children if they need help pick out their outfits and have their backpack ready before going to bed so that the morning routine will flow more timely and effectively. This careful responding helps you notice things you might have neglected had you chosen to react instead of responding mindfully.

So what is empathy if not a way of communicating and connecting better? It lets your kids know that their feelings are valued and taken into account as well, even when the parents don't understand their situation. It is having this knowledge that counts. Empathy suggests that you aren't alone in all this and that we are here for you. It also says that we care and feel for you and wish to make it better somehow.

Receiving this message is important for your kids as they need to hear this. It makes them feel less scared and more confident because they have strong backing. They are no longer reluctant to try something that scares them. They feel more confident in their capabilities, and that is what helps them form good, healthy habits.

Every child wants to know that they are supported and understood. This makes them stay committed and driven to their passions. When they feel that their parents aren't happy with their choices, and often regard them as amateur and senseless, they are soon to give up. Try repeatedly telling a child that playing the guitar won't help them with their grades, and one day, they will give it up. They will start believing what you have been telling them and give up on their dreams. This is one reason why psychologists hate the idea of limiting kids to choose their passions. They may never find out if they are good at something or not if never given a chance.

Secondly, empathy also helps kids become self-aware and speak up for themselves and others. When they see that their parents care and show interest, they are going to act similarly toward others. Empathy is a great quality to nurture from an early age to help children develop into emotionally-intelligent adults.

Empathy also helps one understand the cause of certain behavior. It allows the parent and the child to work as a team to resolve any obstacles together. Not to mention, when your family work as a team, it strengthens your bond and helps you two connect on a deeper level.

Although we shall discuss empathy in great depth in chapter 3, we would like to end this chapter by leaving you with the four important elements of it.

1. *See Things from Someone Else's Perspective:* The first thing empathy entails is putting your feelings and emotions aside and looking at things from someone else's perspective without judgment. Know that no one likes to act out or misbehave on purpose. Even when a child misbehaves out of the ordinary, they are trying to seek attention. This is a call for love. If they are failing at something repeatedly, they aren't deliberately trying to test your patience. They are trying their best but facing some difficulty reaching the result. Empathy is simply knowing that your child is trying their best.

2. *Stop Judging:* Similar to point #1, empathy calls for acceptance without judgment. It stops one from jumping to conclusions right away and understand what is happening.

Most of the time, we lack complete information about something or neglect the signs of distress when we see them. We don't have the time to deal with them, and hence, let things be as they are. Therefore, the second most important thing is to know what more you need to know before giving them a sentence and taking out your frustration on your children.

3. *Understand the Feelings of Others:* In this case, the feelings of your child. You have to tap deep within yourself to understand where your child is coming from. What would you have done had you been in a similar state at a similar age? Your kids, no matter small or big they are, lack the wisdom you have. They may not have everything figured out as you do, and that messes with their brain. As a result, they act out, disobey commands, and misbehave. So if there is a certain way that they are reacting, try to make sense of what they are going through and how they are processing the overwhelming feelings. This also applies to when they are overly excited about something and stop listening to you, perhaps like running in a crowded amusement park when you tell them not to. But chances are, you would have done the same at that age, so what they are feeling is quite normal. It's you who sees it as misbehavior. Maybe they are just being kids.

Communicate Better: Your goal as an empathetic listener shouldn't be to try and fix the problems your kid faces. Maybe all they need is an ear to voice out their fears and not an actual solution. Therefore, avoid trying to take the controls from them and fix things on your own. Let them come to one themselves. All you should offer is some direction. You should just help them express themselves better and encourage them to push through it with supportive words. Use reflective phrases more where you ask them what they think would be the best thing to do in the current situation. Use comforting gestures like hugs, a pat on the back, kisses on the cheeks, and an arm around their shoulder to let them know you care, understand, and worry for them.

Chapter 3: They're Just Little People

Have you ever wondered when we stopped being kids? Did we just wake up feeling different one day? Or, did our "adult" wisdom come to us in a dream? When did so many of us stop being in awe of life and end up with a mundane 9 to 5 to make a living?

If given the opportunity, how many of us would like to go back in time like a glitch in the Matrix and be our younger selves again? Maybe not all of us want to go back to our younger selves, but many of us would agree that we want to live a carefree life. Well, sadly, Rowan and I don't hold any secret codes to a time machine, we are simply curious when do we stop being kids and become adults. When and how did we get over with all the playing and get serious about responsibilities and chores that need to be done?

Not long ago, many scholars believed that kids were nothing but miniature versions of adults. They were regarded to have the same thinking and analytical ability as a fully-grown adult. However, this wasn't true. What was true, though, was that kids were mindful. Their ability to laugh at any situation, be truly indulged in the present, and being honest were all traits that many adults aspire to possess today. Similar to laughter, mindfulness is contagious. We forget all our worries too and enjoy the present moment when surrounded by young children.

So, if the ability to be mindful is something we all had as children, then why can't we be mindful all the time? Why are we stressed 90% of the time about the things that either happened in the past or are too far along in the future? Why can't we just focus on the present and live life to the fullest? It's paradoxical that as we grow "older and wiser", many of us become more disconnected with things and the people around us and become more consumed with constant worries and problems. The life of a parent is not much different either. We are always worrying, planning, running here and there, and focusing on anything but the present. We rarely feel that we are capable of controlling our emotions and prefer to keep them suppressed. As a result, it affects all the relationships we build, even the ones with our kids.

How Are Kids Different From Us?

When we want to learn about the differences between our kids and us, we have to take into account cognitive milestones as they represent the development of a child accurately. As stated before, for many centuries, researchers believed that kids were small adults. It was in the late 20th century that scientists, via several cognitive experiments, figured that there was nothing true about that. The minds of both kids and adults functioned differently. Several attributes differ between kids and adults.

Jean Piaget's contribution to determining the different cognitive developments in kids holds valuable significance. According to Piaget, many life-long habits are learned by kids during their infancy and adolescence stages. Children are born with great thinking and exploring capabilities, which enables them to become curious and discover things on their own. From the minute they are born, they are grasping new concepts, trying to imitate behaviors and actions, and learning from their surroundings. To simplify things, he categorized the cognitive development into four distinct stages which include the Sensorimotor stage (birth to two years), Preoperational stage (from two years to seven years), Concrete stage (from seven years to eleven years), and the Formal Operational stage (from twelve years and beyond).

Mr. Piaget regarded kids as little scientists, always eager to explore the endless possibilities of ideas. Their curiosity and fascination for everyday things and how they functioned was something that held great interest to him, which is why he was such a keen observer of the development of their minds and learned how they used their brains to explore and experience things. He discovered that the more intrigued a child was about something, the bigger their knowledge span was.

In the early stages of cognitive development, all kids portray various personalities because they are used to applying all of their sensory experiences. Their ability to be mindful allows them to engage with world through different modalities fully. When a child reaches the stage of adolescence, they begin to experience many physical and mental changes. Environment and life experiences shape the type of personality the child possesses, which leads us to the Myers-Briggs personality profile—a well-known way of identifying what category of personality type each of us falls under. Let's take a look and learn what your little one's personality is like and see a rough but predictable draft of how they are going to grow up.

Children and Their Distinct Personalities

Many of us believe that babies are born with a clean slate. We feel that whatever we write on that board will be the traits they pick up. All this goes well until the next one arrives, and we feel confused as to why our parenting methods no longer apply to them in the same way they did to the first child. It feels like they have a mind of their own, and nothing we say or do gets imprinted on them. This is when it dawns on us that not every child is the same, and every child has a distinct personality they bring within themselves. We have all labelled our kids resembling someone from the paternal or maternal side in terms of habit with things like, "You are just like your Aunt Judy. She loved to play tennis when she was young ", or "You are growing up to be just like your grandfather. He used to nibble on his food the same way you do."

Therefore, with each child bringing a set of completely different personalities to the table, our parenting games need to be purposeful and strategic. We need to incorporate distinct methods that not only work for both children but also tailor to their unique needs and interests. So, keep this in mind, it is time we assess all the various personality types, so we can better understand our kids.

The Myers-Briggs assessment is divided into eight categories, which further subdivide into sixteen personality types revealing your child's innate profile. It is designed for people of all ages, including adults. Employers sometimes use this assessment for hiring or for placing employees with teams that most suitable for them. Each personality type is represented by four letters paired together, and each letter is a unique characteristic in itself. The following are the eight basic personality types (paired) we shall discuss in greater detail below.

1. Extravert and Introvert
2. Sensing and Intuition
3. Thinking and Feeling
4. Judging and Perceiving

Extrovert and Introvert

To determine where a child's core energy comes from, we look at two variables – external and internal. Are they the ones to come out of their classrooms last, or are they the first ones to burst through the doors, pumped up with energy, and ready to tell you everything that happened that day? Does the thought of going to a cousin's house excite them, or do they prefer to stay back at home? An extroverted child seems always to be on fire and fueled by adrenaline. An introverted kid, on the other hand, will be reluctant to open up or be social. Extroverts are party animals and enjoy the company of others, whereas introverts are less excited about meeting people and often throw tantrums to prevent them from going altogether. Introverts like their own space and frequent changes tend to upset them.

Extrovert

Social interactions energize extroverts. Extroverts are often the kids that get along with everyone they meet for the first time. They are not hesitant to engage in a social setting, and their curiosity to know everything about all subject matter is what makes them such active and action-packed individuals. They strive for chaos and are not ones to be made to sit in a corner and observe others. They want to be included. Their lack of calmness sometimes affects their ability to concentrate, as they are easily distracted. Due to their tendency to get sidetracked, they don't often make for the brightest of students in the traditional academic setting; however, they can achieve greatness if taught things creatively. They enjoy learning that is hands-on and comes with physical engagement. They are more likely to learn in classrooms with fewer students, as it allows them to engage in conversations actively.

Introvert

Introverts are the opposite of extroverts. They are energized by their inner world of thoughts, reflection, and contemplation. They are often average learners and require time and space to do things their way. Many of them love reading and writing, which makes them great students when they are interested in the subject. Their learning style is often suited for traditional classrooms where peers and teachers present them with long lectures. They want to work in a corner and be left by themselves to work on their task. They are rarely open and expressive, but when they are, they prefer it happening one-on-one or a small group. As kids, they prefer discipline and routines, as they find comfort in predictability and consistency. Compared to extroverts, they tend to be more mindful, as they take their sweet time in cultivating responses rather than speaking their mind without thinking.

Sensing or Intuition

An ideal way to determine which personality type your child possesses is to ask them to remember an event or place they recently visited. Notice what they remember about it the most. Is it the ambiance and the mood or the smell, sounds, or colors? See what words they use to describe the event too. Sensing descriptors are more concerned about how the event was carried, and the intuitive descriptors are more concerned about the various elements such as the table decorations, layout, and theme of the place.

Sensing

To be clearer, kids with a sensing personality use all their senses to gather information. They are more receptive and keen observers. They are inspired by visually appealing details and generally are good listeners. They have a good memory and recall things faster. They also like to abide by the rules and play safe. Having a kid with a personality type in this category means you have someone who wishes to adhere to the set rules and regulations and rarely has the urge to challenge them. They also like to have things planned for the whole day, such as knowing the time for a bath, the time to play or nap. They crave structure, concrete facts, and organization in all things.

Intuition

These people use their intuition to guide them through things. They are curious beings and creative. They are, at times, quite hasty as they tend to miss important facts and thus aren't the type to be caged in with rules. Their curiosity keeps them on their toes all day, and they are the ones exploring things and asking questions. They are little innovators and don't always run to their parents or siblings for guidance. They prefer dealing with things on their own and thus will keep on attempting at one thing for hours until they get it right. They are also energetic and more active.

Thinking or Feeling

Does your kid seem to be motivated by facts or emotions? Thinkers are objective. They are ruled by their head instead of their heart and value truth over tact. They think through things logically and reach sane and rational decisions. Feelers, on the other hand, are subjective. They think from the heart and are more empathetic toward others feelings. Feeling people judge situations and others based on feelings and extenuating circumstances. They make decisions based on principles and values.

Thinking

These kids prefer deciding things based on logic. If it is their turn to enjoy the toy, they will snatch it from their friends rather than paying any heed to the feelings of their friend. They need logic and reasoning for everything that a parent says and won't comply with something without one. Although they are great at dealing with problems on their own and finding ways to resolve issues, their impersonal character and lack of empathy and compassion can, at times, come out too firm on people. In school, they are often the ones with strong opinions and need solid reasoning to change their mind. They don't understand the concept of favoritism and aspire to be treated equally. Therefore, even if you tell them that their little sibling needs more attention because they are sick, they are going to try and challenge you at it.

Feeling

As suggested earlier, feelers are gentle and compassionate. They take into account the feelings of others and their own. They make decisions based on how they feel about the circumstances rather than what they think about it. Due to their receptive nature, they are easily hurt by others; however, this doesn't always mean that they set themselves up for failure. Feeling people are great supporter, mentor, and advocate. They are mostly the ones liked by the majority of other people. They get distressed when they sense interpersonal friction and favor harmony.

Judging or Perceiving

Is your child someone who likes structure and order in everything, or is he/she an individual that prefers to go with the flow of things? Kids who fall in the judging category like to plan things out beforehand whereas kids in the perceiving category like to let things go with the flow and are more flexible with unexpected changes. Judging personality in this instance doesn't mean that your child is judgmental. It refers to how your child prefers to deal with day-to-day activity.

Judging

Kids with this personality type prefer to exercise control over everything in their lives. They are less open-minded to change, decisive and well-organized in general. They grow up to become highly responsible adults as they are all about meeting deadlines and having daily action plans. They crave structure in their lives and prefer single-tasking. You have a kid with the judging trait if they watch TV first and later eat dinner because they seek closure and enjoy completing tasks.

Perceiving

Kids who fall under perceiving category are rather spontaneous and prefer not being caged in with any set plans and deadlines. They aren't a big fan of schedules and routines either as they like adventure and spontaneity in life. They like to have all the resources and information they need to make decisions. They grow up to be great at multitasking. Their spontaneity in life makes them good at reacting better in emergencies when things don't go according to the plan. However, the only drawback of their personality is that they are better at starting things but not so much at completing them. They tend to view deadlines as mere suggestions and they like to keep their option opens.

Importance of Personality Analysis

The reason we have provided you with these insights about each personality type is so that you can understand where your children are coming from when they are behaving in a certain way. Although a child's personality should never be the reason for behaving inappropriately, it can be beneficial for parents to understand their nature, so they have a better chance of dealing with them in a much more tactical and calm way. Every child is different, so it can be quite overwhelming for one parent to deal with multiple kids of different ages and different personalities.

For example, a child with an introverted personality may resist going to crowded spaces because they find it hard to mingle like other kids and, instead, opt for a quiet spot in the corner. However, when parents force that child to mingle and get comfortable with other kids, that is where the problem arises. This occurs when the parent isn't concerned about the personality of the child or isn't much aware. However, a conscious parent will be better able to understand the feelings of their child and will avoid forcing them to engage in activities that might deem conflicting the nature of the particular children and instead foster them to grow and develop skills that align with their personality types.

Similarly, if a parent knows that their child is someone who prefers sticking to strict routines, they might not try to upset the children's routines by making swift changes. Instead, they might try to make those changes as subtle as possible so that it doesn't bother their kid or hurt their feelings. We can go on with many more examples, but hopefully, you have understood the memo and see why paying attention to their personality and trying to parent them accordingly can be a tool for better parenting. When the child doesn't feel threatened, pushed or forced into doing something that isn't them, a stronger and healthier relationship can be built.

Enter Mindful Listening

One of the most effective ways to handle tantrums and outrages from kids, without losing your own sense of calm, is to listen to them mindfully so that you don't miss out on the early signs of distress and discomfort. It is always best to run ideas and plans with kids before you try something to implement something novel. For instance, if you want them to clean their room after they are done playing, it is best to address your concern prior. Chances are when kids know what is expected of them; they behave better. We used the same tactic on all of our kids, and trust us, they made less mess knowing they will have to clean up afterwards - before dinner time! If they listen to you and you listen to them, things will run much more smoothly - most of the time.

The art of listening is an underrated one, especially in parenting. However, those who have had more than one child will know what we are talking about. Kids have a mind of their own and, often, many things they say or do don't make much sense. However, when matters are communicated efficiently, and both the involved parties know what the other expected of them, there is less chance of conflict and thus, an even lesser chance of losing your temper.

Listening allows you to give your child your uninterrupted attention when they are telling you things and showing them that you care. It involves using all of your senses to let them know that you are present and you understand them. Your verbal response should align with your body language and the actions you take. Sometimes, it isn't hard for a kid to know that they are being bribed into something and that the parent isn't sincere. False hopes and fake promises are the biggest blunders parents make. Therefore, your actions should also be in line with your words, to show sincerity.

When listening mindfully, you must ensure that you are listening without judgment and with patience. You must also show the utmost interest in the conversation, no matter how senseless it seems. If you aren't mindful, it will be very easy for you to lose focus and become distracted. Half listening to your kid will tell your child that you aren't fully engaged or that their issue does not matter. Not to mention, you might miss out on some important detail that was the essence of the whole conversation. Failing to listen to that means you won't be able to respond empathetically and provide a practical solution for their problem or inquiry.

Did you know that an average person remembers only 25% of what they just heard someone say a few minutes ago (Nichols & Stevens, 1957)? This means that our mind has a tendency to be distracted. If we are not paying attention, important pieces of information might get jumbled up. Now imagine being a parent and being the sole provider, guide, mentor, maid, nutritionist, guard, and companion of someone. Imagine the number of conversations going on in the house and at the office during work. It seems impossible to be handled them all with the same level of attentiveness, right?

We all have limited time and energy in a day. Hence, we must prioritize what is important. We, as parents, should invest time and energy at home as much as we do at work. One reason why kids these days feel less supported is that they think their parents aren't giving them the attention and time they deserve. So often we hear children mention about their parents bringing work home or they are checking work email or picking up work phone even on vacation. Therefore, to avoid your children perceiving you as disinterested in their matters and making your children feel like a second priority to your work, learn to become a mindful listener. Be present in front of your children. Look into their eyes when you communicate with them. When you are present, you can address your children's concerns before they become issues big enough to throw you off your parenting game.

Why do you need to become a mindful listener? Well, the perks are quite convincing. For starters, when you listen to your child mindfully, you allow yourself to be fully in the moment, all ears, which means you can hear the message being delivered to you. You can put a stop to all those wandering thoughts that rush through your mind, giving you a moment of complete solitude. This makes the speaker feel valued, heard, and most importantly, cared for. Mindful listening also allows you to grasp what has been told before passing any judgments. This way you have more time to absorb it all in first and then form a response.

This encompasses more than just hearing something but rather, understanding it. When you listen mindfully, you don't only listen to what has been shared with you but also make sense of the facial expressions, tone, and body language. This can further facilitate a parent to interpret what is being told and then form better and encouraging responses. Finally, mindful listening doesn't involve interruptions in between; the listener is supposed to listen without interrupting the speaker so that the speaker's train of thought isn't broken. Interruptions may cause your children to hesitate and sensor themselves. Thus, they were not able to fully express their conflicting emotions, leading to an emotional build-up that later can be detrimental to their mental and emotional state.

According to Dr. Larissa G. Duncan, an associate professor of Human Development and Family Studies at the University of Wisconsin-Madison, parents who are accepting and aware of their child's needs and wants are far more satisfied with the kind of relationship they have with their child and also tend to avoid cycles of dysfunctional parenting behavior.

Other studies also reveal that mindful listening helps kids handle challenges more effectively and be more compassionate when responding to others (Hanceroglu, 2017). This is something you can and should teach your children from an early age by setting a good example for them. Take a look at what mindfulness looks like when put into practice below.

What Mindful Listening Looks Like

When initiating a conversation, be present physically and mentally. You don't want to make your child think that you are distracted, in a rush, or uninterested. If they sense this, they will stop coming to you with their problems and choose to stay quiet. This will impact the way they communicate with others too. Therefore, remind yourself that once you have committed to hearing them out, they become your #1 priority. Don't let them think otherwise.

Secondly, if you are busy or think that you are too distracted or out of control to have a decent conversation, maybe choose a later time to have it. Again, the idea is to lend them not just an ear but your heart and mind too. Therefore, if you think that this important conversation can take place at some other time or place that is more appropriate, let them know that. However, make it a point to ensure that they know you aren't just shushing them off but rather want to give them your undivided attention.

If you had been distracted or engaged in some other activity like watching TV or looking at your phone, switch it off or set it aside. Nothing will hurt the speaker more when they feel that the listener is not interested in what they are trying to say, and instead distracted by electronic devices. In this case, if your child thinks that you are more interested in your social media updates than you are in them, then they will feel disrespected. It gives them the impression that what they have to say holds little value in the eyes of their parents, and therefore, there is no point in sharing it.

Repeat things but rephrase when needed. In other words, take what your child has said to you, and put them into your own words. When done mindfully, both the speaker and listener feel like they are on the same page. This also helps the speaker know that they have been listened to carefully and that you care about what they've said.

Using your own words to repeat back what has been said also builds understanding between both parties and tells the speaker that they can move on with the rest of their conversation. In simpler terms, it shows the speaker that the message has been received.

Encourage the child to be more open and comprehensive. The more information you have, the more equipped you will be at assessing their condition and coming up with a solution. To encourage them, you don't necessarily have to use words. You can simply smile and nod. You can ask for more information if they seem to be emotionally open to let you in on more (in case they aren't crying). This shows that you are genuinely interested and seeking more information so that you can help them better. It also tells them that their words and concerns hold value, which makes them feel confident and more willing to share.

You two should be on the same physical level. This means if they are standing, you should be too. If they are on the ground, that's where you need to be as well. Don't talk down to them as it could come off as if you are looking down on them. It may also suggest an authoritarian pose, and that is the last thing your kid needs. They are coming to you as a friend, and that is what they should feel like. Aim to maintain steady eye contact with them too. When you two are on the same level, it increases their level of comfort too.

Don't interrupt, but if you do, apologize immediately. Cutting your children off in the middle of a statement by correcting them or offering them advice without hearing them out completely is, again, disrespectful. Allow your children to finish their statement before contributing to the dialogue. Trying not to interrupt your children can be hard when what they are saying does not seem rational to you. However, if you catch yourself interrupting your child, as stated before, apologize quickly and ask them to continue.

Sometimes, we know where the conversation is going. We start to think about possible conclusions. When we have a few ideas in mind, it is very easy to blurt them out without letting the other person finish their thought. This is against the rules of mindful listening. You must, at all times, be patient and let your child say what they are saying even if you have already heard about their dilemmas a thousand times before today. The idea is to encourage them to speak their mind and not act like a know-it-all. Try to stay open-minded and let the tiny speaker finish before suggesting things. Once they are done, take some time to process things and formulate a response accordingly. Even if you have the solution figured out the minute they start the conversation, simply pause before you respond, and take the time to show them that you are genuinely listening and want to help.

Before forming a final response, during that brief pause, repeat all that had been told to you in an inquisitive tone. Keep asking them if you have heard them correctly so that you avoid any misunderstandings. Keep most of your questions open-ended. Asking for more clarity and information by asking open-ended questions is another great way to listen mindfully as it encourages the speaker to go into the depth of things rather than leaving you with surface-level information to form a response. Furthermore, keeping your questions open-ended also means there is room for more dialogue to occur in the future.

Avoid finishing the sentences of the speaker. You want to hear the whole story before contributing your input. You want them to express their concerns without being cut-off in the middle. Completing the sentences of the speaker for them can change the direction of the conversation, and the speaker may feel little control over it. This is both discouraging and degrading.

Stay mindful of your expressions, sensations, and body language. If the conversation is making you feel uncomfortable, it is best not to let your body language deter your children from going into further details. If the conversation is uncomfortable to you, it surely is significantly more difficult for your children to share. The fact that your child musters up the courage to share it to you, the least you could do is to listen and support them. You should stay calm throughout the conversation and think with an open mind, even when you don't agree with half of the things being told to you.

Mindful Listening Techniques for Stressed Parents

Sometimes, the very act of listening is stressful. It involves engagement and concentration and, really, who has the time for it when our schedules are running jam-packed? But it isn't always a lack of time; sometimes we just don't know how to do it. We have an idea of how to listen and what mindful dialogue is; however, to really execute it can be a different story. The initiation and setting for the conversation have to be right so that it doesn't feel staged or forced. It has to happen naturally where the speaker feels welcomed to talk and contribute. Below are three different ways to get the communication going while making it seem natural.

You Go Next...

In this mindful listening exercise, the speaker and the listener set a time of the day to sit down and talk about something. The best time for communication is when both participants feel awake and fresh, calm and attentive. To begin, start by discussing maybe how stressful things have been for you lately, and how tough the work was at the office. The idea is to get them interested first in your own story and then share some of their concerns, too. See if they are willing to contribute and open up with you. If not, ask them if their school is as hectic also. Later, probe further by asking things like if they have to deal with bullying schoolmates or irksome friends similar to your coworker at the office, etc. You get the point.

Make this one-on-one session a routine. Set a few rules, such as one partner gets to say their share uninterrupted for three minutes. Only then can the next partner can share their thoughts and troubles. You can also discuss your relationship, such as what things your child does that bothers or hurts you, and they can tell you what bothers them about you vice versa. This way, you will notice a significant change in their attitude towards you and you both will find yourself with less conflicting opinions than before. Since all kids want to impress and please, they will also avoid deliberately pushing your buttons in an attempt to frustrate you.

Bottle Up…

This exercise involves some craftwork on your part, but hey, you can always have your kid/kids join in and help. This idea comes from the Pixar movie, *Inside Out*, with emotion bottles, each labelled for a different emotion (Marschel, 2019). Since kids aren't always verbal when they are mad and prefer to stay silent, how can you get them talking and listen mindfully to their concerns? Introduce emotion bottles. Make use of empty or old plastic bottles and label each one with an emotion. For "angry," you can add a red solution to the bottle as red usually depicts anger. You can also print out a mad expression or emoji to stick to it. You can have more bottles for "sad," "happy," "excited" or "afraid," etc.

Whenever the child feels an overwhelming emotion but doesn't want to talk about it openly, ask them to pick up an emotion bottle that they can currently relate to. Whichever container they choose will give you various ideas to deal with that emotion. For example, if they select the red bottle, it means that they are angry. Once you know, you have multiple choices. You can either let them have some personal space or try to start a conversation.

You see, this is also a form of mindful listening. It may not involve verbal expression or sharing of issues. It still gives you an overall idea of how to deal with it. You accept their emotions and don't judge them.

Validate Me, Please...

This is more of a tip than an actual exercise and involves the sharing of opinions, without being judged. Validation from parents builds confidence in kids, and they become better at pursuing new things. Validation from kids helps parents know that they are doing their best and raising good kids. So, in a way, it works both ways and benefits everyone in the end.

Again, make it a habit to discuss rather than fight about anything and everything. As a parent, you should aim to get things cleared out verbally in a calm and composed manner to prevent any major dramas and nagging. Let your kids know that you are always there to listen to whatever bothers them. Let them know that they can always come to you with their problems and that you will be all ears without judging their choices.

Promise them that whatever you will offer as a response will be a mere suggestion to improve on the existing idea of something, and not judgment. When you give them advice, be prepared that sometimes your children may not take your suggestions and decide to do their own thing. It can be hard for you as a parent when you know that their ideas and solutions can hurt them, or cause pain, but think of it as a process of trial and error. If it's a minor decision that does not have a long effect or put them in danger and that the lesson from the mistake can be an essential part of your child's development, let your children make that mistake. Even when they do get hurt after doing what they wanted to do, they will still know that you tried to help them earlier and thus would think of turning to you for future advice. That is how you cultivate trust.

Chapter 4: Parents are People Too

Since it all starts with who you are as a parent and what values you want your kid to grow up with, one of the most important aspects of parenting is self-care. Self-care involves taking ownership of your mental, emotional, and physical wellbeing. It is about putting yourself first and giving your body and mind the nourishment it needs. People often are willing to do more for people they care about than they would have done for themselves, and that's a bad mindset to have. Yes, your children are your priority, but you are your children's foundation. If you have a poor self-care habit and you are not able to be your best self, then you are setting a similar example for your children. If you are aware of the negative impact poor self-care can have on you, you will never want your kids to learn bad self-care habits from you. But before we get to that, below is a bit of a pep talk to convince you to give self-care a try.

You Are a Person First

What if we told you that you don't always have to be a parent? What if we told you that you are a person first and then a parent? Parenthood sometimes muddles the difference between the two, and we see both identities as one. But they aren't one. You have to invest in your personal growth, too. Sure, your kid's life seems the most important thing right now, but trust us, they will figure out most of it on their own. They might seek suggestions, but they will be doing most of the work themselves. A lot of parents get so invested in the lives of their kids that they forget to be their own person as well. We all have some physical, emotional, and social needs. Having any of these needs unmet stresses us out. How often has it happened that you just want to leave everything behind and be somewhere new? Of course, your conscience won't allow you to drop everything, but if you are feeling this, it is a sign that you have been neglecting your personal needs for a long time.

Don't get us wrong, there are many perks of becoming a parent, but you have to take care of yourself first. How can you expect to take care of your children and your family if you don't care about yourself? Just an idea to think about for now. The only enemy here is the society which expects us to believe that our life should revolve around our kids only. We fear that we would be perceived as selfish or as "bad parents" if we do something for our own pleasure. Some of us even feel ashamed about wanting to do things for ourselves.

Other parents find it surprising that we even thought about such a thing, but trust us, you don't have to listen to what anyone else thinks. Your health should always be your primary concern. Other people aren't the ones helping you with the kids. They aren't the ones fulfilling family demands. They aren't the ones taking your children to parks when you don't have an ounce of energy left in you. They aren't the ones tending to your kid's needs when they are sick and cry all night. They aren't the ones waking up in the middle of the night, changing diapers, and feeding the infant. YOU ARE! So don't let them bully you into thinking that wanting something for yourself every once in a while is selfish.

You are not committing a sin, if, at times, you feel like fulfilling your needs first and then your kids. You shouldn't be ashamed or feel guilty about asking for some "me" time. It is your right by all means, and everyone around you should respect that.

Self-Care and Its Role in Parenting

Self-care is any activity that results in making us feel whole and improve our well-being, whether it's our mental, physical, and emotional state. It is a way to deal with the exhaustion that comes with everyday work. Since we view parenting as a full-time job, with no sick days, it can become quite monotonous and draining. This is why you must always find the time to invest in yourself and deal with the challenges that come with being a parent. Self-care practices have been associated with reducing stress and alleviating symptoms of anxiety and depression. When we nourish our bodies with the right nutrients, it performs better too.

There are some misconceptions regarding what self-care is and isn't. Before we move onto the practices to self-care, let's have a look at what self-care isn't so that you don't mistake it for something other than looking after one's self.

Self-care isn't forced - but, it is something that we have to be deliberate about in order for it to happen. It's another part of mindfulness. We have to be mindful of how we're feeling and what we need to do to take care of ourselves. It could be as simple as taking a quiet bubble bath, going to the spa, having coffee with friends, and getting out of the house for just a bit. At its core, self-care involves spending your time doing things that make you happy. In the wise words of Agnes Wainman, it shouldn't be something that drains your spirits or energy but rather refuels it.

Secondly, self-care isn't a selfish act. It doesn't mean attending to one's needs without any consideration about anyone else. But, it is about knowing what choices you need to make to take care of yourself so that you can take care of others. If you're exhausted, frustrated, and tired, you can't really be there for other people. As stated before, self-care is nourishment for your body and soul. It stems from the idea that if one doesn't feel cared for, they are less likely in a position to help others. Therefore, you have to fill your own cup first, because you can start filling other people's cup.

Five Areas of Self-Care

One of the most common reasons parents come up with when we suggest self-care practices for reducing frustrations and controlling anger is that they don't have the time for it. Then we bring out the big guns and tell them that they don't need to plan extensively for it, as we aren't suggesting packing your bags and going on a solo journey (although we could). It usually means making the most of the available time you have on your hands when your kids are either asleep or not around. It simply requires some time management skills on your part, and it is completely up to you to decide how much time you are willing to allot for yourself and when.

You start by finding something that truly lightens up your day. It can be an activity or hobby you used to love a while ago or something that adds value to your life, like learning a new skill or doing volunteer work. You might feel like this is not achievable; however, you just have to take a leap of faith and give it a try. You will be astonished by how carving out a little time for yourself daily makes a difference in your day.

There are five different levels or categories of self-care. Each demonstrates a distinct need, and ideally, meeting all these needs should be a priority in your life. The reason we are discussing this in such great depth is that we want you to use these five categories to create a to-do list of activities that fall under each category and start making time for them.

Sensory

Sensory care, as the name suggests, refers to taking care of your sense. Sensory care is the activation of one or more of the senses, including taste, smell, vision, hearing, and touch. It can range from something as simple as a hand massage with scented lotion or listening to a playlist of favorite music to more complicated activities designed to provide a sensory experience. Whatever you do, be present and ensure that you are in a calm and stress-free environment. Practicing mindful sensory care will allow you to focus on the present moment and let go of any limiting or negative thoughts about your past or future.

You should aim to pick activities or interests that involve all of your senses and notice which ones you are most responsive too.

Emotional

Emotional self-care refers to the attainment of stable emotional health. This entails the management of your emotions and how you control them. Again, managing your negative emotions can alleviate stress and symptoms associated with anxiety and depression. Aim for activities that arouse certain emotions and see how you react to them. You can engage in activities that enhance your mood, or you can even attempt things that make you angry, sad, or guilty. Intentionally provoking negative feelings will help you recognize your physiological response to these emotions, subsequently helping you to learn to manage them better over time and not become overwhelmed by them. As a parent whose goal is to avoid unleashing anger and frustration on our child, emotional self-care can be a great way to achieve this.

While trying out the activities that you are unhappy or angry, know that they aren't always bad. Had you never experienced those emotions first-hand, you would have never noticed what pure joy or happiness felt like. Therefore, stop looking at negative emotions as something bad or unwanted and embrace and accept them as they come.

Social

Social self-care involves a connection with others to share your happiness, concerns, and grief with. We tell our clients to view it as something of equal importance as our physical needs because social support is crucial to our well-being. It doesn't matter if you are an introvert or extrovert; we all have a few close friends or partners we are comfortable opening up to. The goal should be spending quality time with them and talking about things that affect you – both positively and negatively. Additionally, it takes off some of the pressure that comes with parenting, and you see that you aren't the only one facing challenges. Sharing your experiences with other parents may help you realize that you are not the only person experiencing the issues you are facing with your children. Maybe other parents may have an effective solution or helpful advice for your problems.

Spiritual

Know that spirituality doesn't only have to do with believing in a deity, nor is it necessarily tied to religious practice. Paying attention to our spiritual health involves getting in touch with our core values, cultures, and traditions as well. It is about doing things that are fulfilling and help us see ourselves as part of humanity. It is about feeding your soul, rather than just your mind or body, with what matters to you the most. Some people prefer practicing spirituality through meditation, chanting, journaling, etc. Others may prefer something more socially interactive, like doing yoga, joining local hiking group and spending time in nature, volunteering in the community etc. If you care about elderly people, you may choose to volunteer at a nursing home. Spiritual practices do not need to be related to any religious tradition. You are simply doing good for the sake of good. There is no hidden agenda, and you aren't pretending to do something you are not interested in. So in a way, it is more about finding a purpose in your life that makes your life meaningful and connected to humanity.

Physical

Finally, we have physical self-care, which refers to taking care of your body through adequate sleep, healthy and nutritious food (for you and your family), exercising, and staying fit. You'll find that when you take care of your body, your body takes care of you. When you eat in an overall healthy way, you have much more energy to spend quality time with your family and with yourself. You will also be modelling healthy habits and healthy relationships with food by keeping things in moderation and sticking with a generally healthy lifestyle.

Best Self-Care Strategies for Busy Parents

The second you become a parent, your whole life seem to revolve around looking after your little bundle of joy. It is very natural to lose sight of your own needs and put theirs first. But as stated before, you can't keep suppressing your needs for a long time as this can only result in more frustration and exhaustion on your part. Therefore, here are some great self-help strategies ideal for parents to ensure they don't neglect their personal needs. Because at the end of the day, you have to take care of yourself so that you can be a better parent for your little human.

Meditate

Meditation, even if it is for a few minutes every day, can allow you to stay rejuvenated. With so many guided meditation apps and online videos, you no longer have to learn how to do it but simply follow the advice. Even five minutes of daily meditation can help clear your mind and relieve your body of any worries and problematic thoughts. It can serve to be the perfect start to your day and keep you calm and your mind less cluttered.

Take a Digital Detox

We are so used to picking up our phones every few minutes, browsing social media apps so mindlessly, and spending way too much time surfing through the many channels on our TV or laptop that we don't even realize how self-harming that is. Addiction to phones is a real thing, and we have little idea of how drastically it is affecting our health and immune systems. Think about it, when was the last time you put your phone down and left it there for hours at a time? Even in the middle of the night, if we wake up to tend to our kids, we also pick up our phones to check for any new notifications on it.

What also tends to happen is that we expose ourselves to a lot of negativity when we're online, either via our phone or computers. We often see headlines filled with negative news that show society at its worst. Subconsciously, this can stress ourselves out. Rowan and I have a mutual friend who spends most of their day watching and reading political news. And guess what? He's almost always angry and upset. He talks about politics all the time, and how this congressperson does this and that party does that. Over time, this not only affects his daily mental state but his social interactions with others. It changes his interactions with his wife and his children. His family feels that his political anger and frustration was unintentionally misdirected towards them on multiple occasions.

What we suggest is a detox or cleanse. Start with limiting the amount of time spent on your phones and computers. Whenever you're tempted to take a sneak peek, engage yourself elsewhere. You don't have to reply to every message right away or reply to work emails outside of office hours. Keep in mind, also, that the blue light of your cell phone can disrupt your normal sleep cycle—the light halts the production of melatonin, which is the chemical that induces sleep.

Practice Mindfulness

This has been emphasized enough already. We feel like if we talk about it any further, you will close the book and review it as repetitive. However, we just want to let you know that the reason we keep reminding you about mindfulness is that it has been a game-changer, at least in the lives of many people who have come to us seeking parenting advice. Try to focus on your present and let go of the worries that keep you awake at night about your children. They are going to do just fine and with mindfulness in practice, and make better decisions for themselves as they grow older. So, savor what you have today and cherish every moment you have with your toddler. Soon you are going to miss these tantrums and their constant need for you to tend to them.

Start Walking

Walking or brisk walking has a significant impact on our mind and body. For starters, it releases the happy endorphins in our system, which combat stress and worry. Then, it also serves as a means to energize your body and an excuse to enjoy the outdoors for a breath of fresh air. If you have a little one to take care of, how about putting them in a stroller and going for a little walk to the park?

Enjoy Some "Me" Time

We talked about this, as well, in relation to self-care. Doing something just for yourself so that you have the energy and positive attitude to tackle whatever life brings. It could mean lighting up some scented candles, having a glass of wine, and gifting yourself a relaxing bath to release all the negative thoughts and fatigue from your system. It is important to enjoy some time on your own so that you can use that to ponder over the things bothering you. You can also use that time to simply let go of any negative energies from your body by listening to guided meditations or songs that calm you down. The goal should be to unwind in that time of brief solitude and think about your personal goals and the means to achieve them. Indulge in self-motivating thoughts such as where would you like to see yourself ten years from now and visualize how good your life will be. You will instantly feel happiness settling in as that picture of you enjoying a vacation in the Bahamas comes to mind. You can also use that time to charge your batteries and before getting back to playing the role of a parent to your kid.

Interact More

Social connections are another important aspect of self-care. No matter how packed your schedules are, you have to make time for your partner, family, and friends. Not because they are important but because it is important for your mental health. Being a parent can be exhausting. Finding a little time to laugh and share stories with like-minded people can have a positive impact on your mood and psychological wellbeing. Parents, especially mothers, need this the most. Make sure to take out some time to spend with friends and family so that you can get your mind off anything that might be stressing you, and indulge in some carefree time with your pals and family.

Have a "Not To-do" Checklist

With endless thoughts running through your mind all day, checklists can sometimes be super helpful. Be it a recital your child has been preparing for all week or a doctor's appointment you can't miss, having a checklist eases things for both parents. First, they serve as reminders of important events, chores, and dates. Secondly, they also list when all those things need to be done. However, many parents try to squeeze too much into a single checklist, thinking they will be able to get them all done in a day. But here's the thing. No two days are the same when you are a parent to a little one. Who knows what's running in their little mischievous minds. Therefore, to not set yourself up for disappointment, have a checklist with limited chores for a day. Better yet, create a not-to-do list of all those items you don't have to do on your own and can easily be postponed or delegated. For instance, you don't have to go shopping for groceries with a child who doesn't like shopping. You can ask your partner to help out and pick some things up on their way home.

While you're at it, aim to single-task instead of multitasking. Your goal shouldn't be to get more things done but to get the most important things done, and done right. The idea is to stay organized.

Start Journaling

Creating a journal and saving your most precious memories is a great way to release the stress that comes with parenting at times. Some days, we are bound to feel like a failure as nothing goes as planned. For instance, we remember the time we went camping with the kids. Despite taking all the necessary precautions we could have imagined, one kid came back with an infection and the other with a cut on their foot. In those moments, we might feel like such a failure at parenting as these were the things we could have easily avoided. However, when we reflect on the event a few days later, we might feel like we were being too hard on ourselves, and there was very little we could have done to avoid all the camping mishaps. Besides, the kids had a great time and still cherish the moments.

Coming back to the original point, keeping a gratitude journal has been linked to improved sleep quality in adults. It also becomes a way to push out negative emotions because recalling all the good things in life is a guaranteed mood booster.

So make it a habit to keep a gratitude journal and write three things you are thankful for, each day before going to bed. These can be small things like a sweet interaction with one of your children, to big things like a supportive husband, loving kids, and a beautiful home. That way, you will worry less about the stuff that are out of your control and focus on all the good things you have.

What Are You Responsible For as the Parent?

This brings us to another important aspect of parenting; what role do you play as a parent. What are your responsibilities as a provider for your kids? Since we are bombarded with mixed messages daily on the "right" way of parenting, we must understand what our kids need us for and what are the things that they can take care of on our own. So, before you take advice from online strangers or relatives about the things that worked for them and what didn't, take a look at the role we think you have to play as a parent and stop comparing ourselves with others.

What Your Responsibilities Are...

Make Decisions that Seem Harsh

Yes, we said it! Did you know we think that we are not doing our jobs right as parents if our kids don't get angry with us at least once a day? It is your job to keep them safe, and if they don't understand it, then maybe you have to set some ground rules in practice. Of course, those aren't going to make your little one delighted but surely leave you with the comfort of knowing that they are safe and sound.

This also refers to stopping your children's attempts at misbehavior and letting them know that certain behaviors are not acceptable. They should know not to cross the line. If they are watching TV all day and not doing homework, it is your job to turn off the TV and get them to study. They may cry, scream, and whine, but don't let that melt your heart. Whatever you do, you do it to establish discipline and good habits in them.

Teach Independence

Independence doesn't mean you leave them to do the chores and lay on the sofa all day. As their parent, it is your job to train them to attempt child-appropriate skills so that they can refine these skills as they grow older. Kids who stay cocooned throughout their lives suffer from low self-esteem and poor confidence as they are so used to having things done for them. But if you won't let them play in the dirt, you can never expect them to learn anything on their own. They will grow up physically, but their mental and social skills won't. Therefore, make it a habit to teach them skills they should know to do on their own from an early age. That way, they will grow up to become independent, manage their own needs, and attain age-appropriate maturity in their lives.

Sleep training is a great example here. It involves training the child to soothe themselves back to sleep when they wake up in the middle of the night and cry for their parents. Parenting experts suggest that parents should start the training as early as six months so that the child learns to do it themselves. Similarly, at a certain age, your kids should know how to change into appropriate clothes, tie their laces, brush their teeth, and comb their hair, for example. You want to teach them basic life skills that get more advanced as the child gets older. That's the best way to ensure that you've raised your child to be a self-reliant, independent adult.

Set Consequences for Questionable Behavior

It is your responsibility to hold your child accountable for their actions and behaviors. This entails setting consequences for questionable behavior and setting certain limits so that they learn to behave well and abide by the rules set for them. They should, at all times, know that you are not a friend to them who will overlook their wrongdoings. They should know the house rules and that if they break the rules, there will be repercussions.

Accept Stuff as it Happens

There will be days when your little one does everything right, eats well, sleeps on time, and avoids misbehaving. But there will also be days when every little thing they do are opposite of what you wanted, giving you a tough time with eating, throwing tantrums over the sleep schedules, and get on your nerves all day. Those are the days when you don't have to lose your mind or blame yourself for being a bad parent. Instead of blaming and feeling guilty, find ways to cope with the challenges, and accept your child's negative mood and behavior. Your responsibility is to help them steadily navigate through their emotions, not lose your mind.

Pick Your Battles

Many times, parenting feels like being in the circus trying to perform a balancing act on the back of a horse running in circles. You feel lost and are constantly stressing out about whether the consequences of an action should be soft or harsh. This is the time when you need to evaluate which battles are worth fighting and pick them wisely. While doing so, keep in mind that you aren't striving to be the perfect parent, but rather a loving, effective parent.

There is no Shame in Seeking Advice

Finally, if you still feel that you lack the knowledge or resources you need to raise your kids in a healthy and stress-free environment, there is no shame in knocking at someone's door. We often sense the guilt and shame in the eyes of parents who come for help from us. They ask us to keep it confidential because if someone in their family friends found out, it will be embarrassing for them. True, parenting is something that deems to come naturally, but if someone you know is seeking some help, there is no need to shame or blame them. They are simply eager to know of better techniques to deal with child-related issues, and there is nothing wrong with that. It shows that they are truly concerned parents and want nothing but the best for their kids.

Now that we have gotten that all cleared up let's talk about some of the sources where you can receive sound advice and implement it with your kids.

Family: Your parents did a great job raising you, didn't they? If they did, then they are usually the first ones you can turn to when you need help. However, sometimes we don't want them to poke in our parenthood too much. Their views on parenting style may differ, as times are changing, and we want to raise kids differently. Despite that, they have still raised kids on their own and do have a few good tricks up their sleeves. Don't feel ashamed or embarrassed asking them for assistance and guidance whenever you feel like you are in dire need of some support with raising the kids.

Friends: Like family, friends can also be a great source of information and advice, especially if they have kids too. The reason they can be a great source of guidance is that they are easier to talk to and discuss things with because they have probably encountered similar issues with their kids too.

Teachers: In some ways, a good teacher can be an incredible source of information since they deal with dozens, maybe even hundreds of students every day. Many teachers have worked with hundreds, if not thousands of children throughout their career. You can bet they have some good ideas, and they also know your students in a different setting, so they might be able to give a unique perspective.

Online Parenting Groups and Forums: If you still feel reluctant to share your worries with someone that you know, there is always the option of turning to the internet for advice. If we just talk about a single platform, there are thousands of parenting groups and discussions that you can become a part of to stay in touch with all those people going through the same challenges with their kids. However, don't start trusting everything you read online blindly as some of the information might be wrong.

Parenting Resources: Since it is the age of the digital media, you can turn to many audio and online books on Amazon on parenting too. They, too, are aimed at making the process of parenting stress-free and enjoyable.

Parenting Support Groups: Like book clubs or addiction support groups, there are also many parenting support groups to help new parents ease into the transition from a spouse into a parent. Weekly discussions are held regarding child behavior, challenges with disabled and special-needs children, and how to keep one's emotions under control. You can also be an active member and voice your concerns and receive accurate advice from the experts. If you don't have the time to show up every week, you can simply join them when they hold workshops and seminars of your interests with parenting experts as facilitators.

Parent Counselors: Parent counselling is another viable and resourceful option when dealing with kids. Parenting counsellors help struggling parents understand where the issues are coming from to get to the root cause, and what steps must be taken to manage them. They are like mentors who have the knowledge and expertise required to raise good and disciplined kids.

Remember the saying, "It takes a village to raise a child"? Although we may not have the leverage to raise a kid in close-knitted family structures, we still have the power of more knowledge than ever before. There are many resources; between books, support networks, and your friends and family. Take that information with an open heart and mind. Sometimes it means you will have to go out of your comfort zone. So, don't be scared when you feel like you have hit a roadblock. Let your intuition guide you and give you the strength and means to tackle any problem at hand. Be mindful of your actions and responses to critical situations so that you don't do something you'll regret later.

Chapter 5: Taking Ownership of Parenthood

There is hardly a moment when we are anything but a parent to our kids. They are solely dependent on us for every little thing. You are their primary provider. You change their clothes, make them take a bath, play with them, wipe their bottoms, clean up after them, and help them take a nap… The list goes on and on. New parents often see this role as rather permanent. They think that is how their life will be forever from now on. But the role changes with time.

True, taking care of a little child feels like you are all in until the end, but as the kids begin to grow older, their needs for you change. During the first two years, your child might need you for everything, but by the time they turn three or four, they require less assistance with things and want to to try things on their own. They may request to eat from a plate with a fork and spoon like their parents or want to be given a choice to choose what they want to wear. What seemed to be an eternal job begins to feel like a temporary one. By the time they turn eighteen, your children are less physically dependent on you and their needs for you may be more of emotional and social ones. For some parents, it is a hard pill to swallow as they are so used to being the primary caretaker. Transferring the reins into their children's hands can be difficult.

It's fascinating how, during our child's infancy, we keep complaining about wishing to have a glass of wine without being interrupted by the child for once or to be able to chat with our friends at a party without having to change diapers and run after our kids to ensure they stay safe. Then comes a day when we finally get that glass of wine in our hands and a bunch of people to talk to, but our mind remains focused on that little kid that ran away into the other room to play with the other kids their age. Yes, we as parents are quite complicated this way. When we don't have the freedom we want, we crave it, and when we finally begin to get it, we miss being wanted. Parent identities change with time, and it is a fact that kids need less of us as they are growing up.

This is what life with growing kids looks like.

Welcome to it!

The physical demands of kids change. They are mostly replaced by emotional ones. They change from simply cooking food for them to discussing issues with them, talking about their day at school, their friends, academics, and interests and likes. Kids develop an interest in things like sports, arts, and crafts, dancing, or playing instruments, and many of the discussions change, from what they should wear to what they want to wear to an annual event. Thankfully, there is little cleaning to do as the kids finally stop throwing food around or playing with it. It's bittersweet, but also great.

Parents, who we have worked with, report that as their children grow older, they have more free time for self-care and personal activities. They also mention increased productivity at work and improvement in overall mood as they have one less thing to worry about or invest their energy on. Many parents also state that they can juggle work and life better as the kids need less parental involvement in everything they do.

Our expectations as parents further evolve, as well. Many women, especially those who work, have shared with us that they feel more comfortable in taking on challenging projects since they now have the freedom to give their work the time it deserves.

When kids enter their teen years, the conversations and dynamics of the relationship once again change. However, it greatly depends on how much the kid trusts their parents. If they know that they will be judged and ridiculed when they come to you for advice, the relationship will be less than comfortable. Similarly, if they know that they won't be judged or ridiculed, the relationship will be more connected and stronger. The conversations change from friends to crushes and higher studies prospects. The interests change from building tree houses to full-time careers and apprenticeships.

In a nutshell, the role of a parent evolves with time, and it is solely on us to make the best of those changes. Keep in mind, as a parent, your foremost job is to be their mentor and friend so that you both are comfortable sharing ideas and talking about anything and everything. Mindful parenting plays a crucial role in that, and this is why we keep chanting the mantra over and over again.

How Mindfulness Helps Manage an Adolescent's Nuances

In a survey from the American Psychological Association, teenagers report the highest levels of stress than any other cohort of humans (Bethune, 2014). The uncertainty about the future and not having a defined identity leaves them in immense pressure, which usually goes unaddressed. The same research also reports that sixty per cent of teenagers don't know how to manage their stress. They mostly turn to the internet for comfort, and upon glancing at the "wonderful" lives of others, it leaves them further unmotivated and stressed.

Therefore, as their parent, it is your job to help them overcome the stressful emotions and learn to manage them from an early age. This is where mindfulness comes into play. Teaching about mindfulness from an early stage helps kids develop emotional-intelligence – the art of managing their emotions as they come and not let the negative ones overwhelm them. However, if you have missed out on the memo and have a child in his teenage years struggling to make it past every day due to existential crisis or a lack of direction, it is still not too late to start with mindfulness exercises.

Teens mostly see the world as black or white. They either think that something is achievable, or it isn't. They feel a wide range of strong emotions, like fascination, regrets, anger, and sadness, a majority of the time. Because their sense of self is still developing, they also prone to low self-esteem issues and poor confidence levels; things essential for their mental health. And the worst part, they are less expressive of complex emotions than they used to when they were kids. They sometimes prefer seclusion and being left alone to deal with things on their own. Many teens subscribe to what can be described as a fixed mindset, which suggests that a person is born with all their talents and skills, and can't really develop new skills, so there is no point in trying or making an effort. Instead, they should foster a growth mindset, and with mindfulness, you can help develop that in them.

Mindfulness teaches them to be more expressive and communicative. It doesn't promote suppressing or ignoring emotions. It makes their mind better at stepping back and processing things better and knowing how to respond to them more adeptly. Again, this takes us back to responding instead of reacting, which we talked about in an earlier chapter. Mindfulness is beneficial for teenagers who have trouble handling increased responsibilities at school, have high expectations from their family and peers, have gone through some emotional break-ups, or pose symptoms of mental health problems due to stressful social environments, arguments with parents or due to some mood disorders.

Below are some great tips for teaching your children mindfulness in a comfortable manner that doesn't seem too forceful, and urge them to adopt these habits for their benefit.

Why Do They Need It?

Being notorious rebels, your teenager will need evidence to decide on a course of action, and that is what you need to give them. You don't have to run after them talking about how great it is for them or how it is going to change their lives. Instead, hand them the resources so that if they feel like it, they give them a try themselves. Keep in mind that you can't make them follow something blindly because they need solid backing and reasoning. Lucky for you, the internet is filled with valuable insights, case studies, and research and implementation information regarding mindfulness. Gradually, introduce them to the many practices and motivate them to give them a try.

Let them know of the benefits that solely connect to them. For example, they are less likely to show interest if you quote benefits like soul enlightenment or self-actualization. However, they will be more intrigued if you put forward benefits like how it can help them perform better in their exams (Mrazek, Franklin, Phillips, Baird, & Schooler, 2013), how it can improve their concentration (Sanger & Dorjee, 2015) and how it can alleviate the stress and anxiety (Marchand, 2012) related to their studies. These are the kind of benefits that they resonate better with. Therefore, be strategic.

Model Mindfulness

Secondly, you have to lead by example yourself. You can't expect your kids to develop good habits when they don't see them in you. If you want them to practice mindfulness, you have to be their teacher. Model it yourself so that they don't have to look elsewhere. They will note the positive changes within you and take it up themselves. This is how you preach. This means that we have to handle stress efficiently without it letting affect us or the lives of others. It also means that we respond wisely and with reason in every situation, no matter how frustrating or agitating it seems. It also means that we stop judging others over their personal choices and accept the opinions of others without remorse or animosity.

Moreover, you can try to teach them via different exercises that involve more than one person, and demonstrate how life-changing it can be for them as well. If they are lucky enough to pick up on the benefits early on and begin to practice mindfulness, then they have a better chance of carrying on these practices in their adult life and being good parents for their own children. The point is to help them see mindfulness in action, and they also need to see that it isn't something complicated. When we sometimes talk about it with parents, they see it as something stressful and time-consuming. But if you have been reading the book and studying the various exercises and tips we have discussed, you would know how simple it is to practice mindfulness.

Teach Them About the Mind

To fully embrace mindfulness, they need to be made aware of how it works as well. Here's a suggested example to explain the concept of mindfulness to your children and how mindfulness affects the mind. Imagine your mind is like the mind of a monkey. Imagine it climbing from one branch onto another. That is how the mind moves from one thought to another. A lot of the stress we feel, whether it is due to our academics, relationships, or worries about our careers, most of it is in our heads only. Our mind is an improviser. It is designed to overthink and project possible conclusions. Without mental training, we have little control over it. So whenever we are stressed, it makes the problem appear bigger. Worrying further adds to our anxiety about things.

However, when we introduce mindfulness into the equation, it helps us see that most of the chatter in our heads is nothing but senseless chattering. We train our minds not to overthink and make scenarios worse. We stop worrying so much about the future as we learn to focus on the present. Mindfulness makes us aware of our thought process and gives us the leverage to practice control over it. This helps us determine which worries are worth stressing about and which are mere projections our mind has created. This way, we can manage our emotions and minimize the damage misdirected emotions can do if left unaddressed.

Owning Up to Parenthood

Your child is a child after all. They are sometimes going to be stubborn and belligerent. They will refuse logic, cry over small things, and plead in front of you to get what they want. You have two choices here — either you give in to their demands and be the likeable parent they want you to be or guide them into the behavior you want them to follow. Many parents opt for the former because it is so much easier and more comfortable, especially when we don't have an ounce of energy left in us.

When interviewing parents, a great number of them think that disciplining via punishment is the best way to instil obedience in kids. In some ways, this is correct; disciplining is indeed the right way, but how the disciplinary action is executed may vary. What some parents have gotten wrong is the definition of the term discipline. Discipline comes from a Latin word which, surprisingly, doesn't mean scolding or spanking. In fact, its literal meaning is "to teach." Disciplining involves showing them right from wrong. It means teaching them how to get over their mistakes and focus on the present. It means letting them know that every action has a good or bad consequence, and therefore, they should think and act wisely.

We have been introduced to an idealized version of parenting. We think that children are supposed to do exactly as told the minute we tell them too. They have no autonomy when it comes to making decisions on their own, and only their parents can decide the best for them. However, this is authoritarian and thus not feasible long-term. Kids who grow up in such households fail to develop a sense of individuality and often don't excel in school or careers. They usually have significant self-esteem issues and find it harder to connect with others and develop meaningful relationships. They lack autonomy until reaching a certain age in their lives. They also often act out irrationally and hesitate in taking orders and are prone to procrastinate and do the opposite of what they have been told. Rebellious, aren't they?

Toddlers cannot internalize hierarchy. They don't have the emotional maturity to regulate emotions and act maturely and sensibly. But that doesn't mean the disciplining in terms of verbal and physical abuse is the answer to their misbehavior. Instead of being strict, we should aim to set clear and well-defined guidelines to help pave their way to doing the right things.

Kids are known to act out for attention. They purposely test your limits by doing something naughty because they know that it is the quickest way to get your attention. Therefore, what we need are structures and preventive training. This means that we have to devote our time and energy into teaching them, with love and patience, and giving them our undivided attention whenever needed. This way, they will stop seeing us as authoritative, and more as a coach; they will gladly want structures and healthy boundaries, and they'll better learn how to be productive members of the family. They will come to know which behaviors are encouraged and rewarded and, therefore, must be adopted and which ones come with negative consequences and, therefore, must be avoided. It has to start with a laid-out structure in the form of schedules and routines which aren't rigid, but consistent enough that your children know what to anticipate and help them stay in line.

Discipline means leading by example and not by punishment or scolding. If only there was a single way to discipline kids, our lives would have been much easier. But since every child is unique in their ways, we have to adopt different ways that resonate with them. Preferably, it should begin by showing empathy, knowing their thought processes, and knowing how those thoughts turn into behaviors. Secondly, mindfulness also plays a crucial role, and so does emotional intelligence. We have to learn to criticize their behaviors and not them. We have to stop scaring them with the thoughts of punishment and educating them about ways to deal with their anger and frustration. At the end of the day, you don't want them to obey you out of fear or resent you for being so stern.

Take Ownership

Just because you love your kids dearly and are ready to give your life for them doesn't mean you let them run the show. They need to know who is in charge at all times. Parents who have a difficult time taking charge often report chaos in their homes with disobedient kids who have no respect for the words of anyone but their own. As their parent, you shouldn't give in to all their senseless and absurd demands, moods or whims. Many parents simply take the back seat because they don't know anything better to do. They feel like a captive spending life in a closed cell, waiting for their kids to grow up and leave.

But it doesn't have to be like this. You don't have to feel like a captive in your own house in front of the kids that you raised and looked after. You have to familiarize yourself with the concept of ownership, and own parenthood like a king or queen. Owning parenthood refers to taking complete charge and responsibility for who you are as a parent and how you are going to raise them. If you ever feel trapped against the whims and actions of your child, feel stuck in between love and discipline, then it is time you own your right as parents and be ready to take charge. Below is a brief description of what ownership of parenting looks like.

Take Ownership of Your Choices

We, as parents, make numerous decisions in a day. Some of them are good and others, not so much. But that is how we grow and learn. We are supposed to act all strict and disciplinary, or society calls us out for being vulnerable. This is the part where we try to hide behind the idea of perfectionism and call out others when they fail at something. But there is no point blaming the society, culture, or our upbringing when most of our circumstances is our own doing. We make our own choices when it comes to parenting. Sometimes we make the wrong choice. Some of us may have a hard time accepting our wrong decisions. Being parents, we have to stand up to the poor choices we made and accept the outcome with some compassion for ourselves. Owning up to our pitfalls and weaknesses is a sign of strength. It is the only way that we can learn to make better choices.

Take Ownership of Your Shortcomings

It can be quite painful to live up to the consequences of any wrong choices or decisions you made, but you have to own up to them. You have to face how those poor choices affected you and your kid and learn to be more aware and prepared in the future. You don't have to be too harsh on yourself as it is all a process of learning. When you humbly accept that you made a mistake that resulted in upsetting the family dynamic, you are being a parent and a great role model for your kids. There is no competition to be the best, and your kid isn't your enemy. Therefore, there shouldn't be any shame associating with learning from mistakes. Admit that what you did was wrong and that you could have done better. When your kid sees qualities like acceptance, letting go, and moving on rooted deep in you, they will strive for the same. When you admit your shortcomings, you allow yourself another chance to change your behavior and create a better future.

Chapter 6: The "Role Model:" Lessons Your Kid Can Teach You

Children aren't born with social skills or social knowledge, so they look up to us and imitate the actions and behaviors of the adults around them. Parents are the first teachers and role models children look up to for guidance and mentorship. Ever notice how accurately our kids pick up some of our habits (good and bad) like chewing food with their mouths open or sitting like their fathers? Where did they learn them from, if not from you? Kids are affected by what they see their parents do. They pick up on behaviors from us and often give us a clear reflection of who we are.

A child's dependency on their parents grows when they begin to make sense of their environments and pick up on our actions. This is the phase where we need to display ethical and moral behavior suitable for them to grow up with. This is also the time when we need to impart strong values such as not losing heart, trying their best, being honest, and being respectful, etc. We also need to prepare them to handle their emotional outbursts with calmness and counter any negative emotions using the presence of mind.

Kids view parents as people they admire, and they want to emulate us. Being their role model, we can inspire them to develop good qualities and habits, along with detailed instructions. Since a child spends the majority of their time with their parents, it is our job to ensure that whatever they are taught adds value to their lives and will help them in their future. These direct interactions are quite meaningful for both the parents and the kids, but can also be a little draining. After all, you have to be your best at all times. It can be hard to keep our chins held high and in full spirits even when we feel down and broken from the inside, at times.

The Stress That Comes With Being a Role Model

At times, the weight of being a parent is hard to carry. We have to be their caretaker, teacher, nurse, friend, and playmate on top of being their parent. Playing all these roles at once can take a toll on even the most experienced parent. We don't want them picking up bad habits, and neither do we want them to think that misbehaving is acceptable. We have the responsibility to preach wellness and improvise when we need to. Being a role model means there is little room for errors, as children are quick learners. Not to mention, the fear of getting something wrong can feel no less than a nightmare for new parents. The best way to deal with the everyday stress that comes with parenting is to become a mindful parent. Mindful parenting opens doors for improving behaviors and submitting to the things as they are happening. We have to accept things first to change them. Lack of acknowledgement can lead to poor decision-making because we react rather than respond.

During various surveys and interviews with children of all ages, we asked how they perceive a role model and whether they regarded their parents as one or not. Surprisingly, the majority of the kids held their parents with great respect and believed that they had a significant influence on their upbringing. We also had a couple of kids depicting symptoms of depression, poor self-esteem, and aggression. Upon some probing, we came to know that the children were modelling certain behaviors after their parents. When this happens, it becomes difficult for us to show them that they can have an identity of their own. It's a hard process but achievable, as we have to teach them to let go of those negative habits first, and later take up good ones. Therefore, as parents, you have to make the most of the time you have with your kids and try to teach them things that benefit them in building their identity.

Since everything seems too complicated, we get how stressed you feel. But you don't have to, especially if you want to instil good habits in them and teach them to adopt mindfulness. Why do we say that? It is because we have worked with many kids and come to the conclusion that kids are mindful by nature. They are curious little beings, love to stay in the present moment and savor everything that comes their way. What better definition of mindfulness is there than that?

Wait, what are we suggesting, you might ask? Hear us out. We are proposing to not view our children as kids but rather role models. Yes, the role has to be reversed. We are suggesting you turn into a student instead of the teacher and pick up all the natural and positive habits children are born with to learn a few things about mindfulness.

Can Our Kids Be Our Role Models?

Have you ever considered that when kids yearn for our attention and interrupt us while we're "doing something important," they aren't trying to distract you but rather bring you back into the present moment? They are forcing you to let go of your train of thought and experience what the now feels like. Since they are born with mindfulness, they can tap into that deep untarnished wisdom that we sometimes lack. When they call upon us to gain our attention, they simply want us to live what they are living and know how good it feels to be immersed in the present moment. They are a good example of how to live life to the fullest. They teach us things we have long forgotten, things that mattered. Take a look at some of the many things they teach us every day. These are habits and behaviors we can learn something from and adopt to enjoy life to the fullest as well.

A New Day is Here

A new day means new opportunities and new adventures. Even if the last one didn't go as planned or wasn't as exciting as promised, kids view the coming dawn as a unique chance to make it better. To them, tomorrow is like a fresh start, a clean slate and a blank canvas on which they can paint with whatever colors they like. They forget about the mistakes they made yesterday and focus on what lies ahead of them today. As adults, we should have the same energy within us. We should feel the same zest and zeal as they do upon waking up. We should see every day as a new opportunity to learn, explore, stumble, and then rise again.

Savor Each Moment to the Fullest

Ever noticed how sometimes children will stay engaged in one thing until they get it right? They aren't the ones to give up easily. They tend to soak in all the beauty around them and use their good time to notice even the most insignificant of things in their surroundings – things even we don't notice anymore. They will go out and gaze upon the sky and smile as if it is the first time they are looking at it. They will run after the butterflies and not stop until they have had a good view of it. They will take hours to finish the six peas on their plate because they have so much happening around that is way more interesting than those peas.

As parents, we often lose sight of the present and rush to get more done in little time. Everything we do is timed. We wake up at a certain time daily, head to the office to clock in at a certain time, then leave and return home, have dinner at a fixed time and then go to sleep at a predetermined time too. Everything in our lives can feel robotic, and we have made it that way. We have forgotten how to savor moments and live them as they are happening. If we think that doing more now will leave us with free time later, then let's pop this imaginary bubble of yours - right here, right now. Responsibilities will never leave you. There will always be something "more important" coming up, so why not focus on what we have today? At his moment?

Accept Things As They Come

Had the "worst day" of your life? Accept it. Didn't make it to the gym? Accept it. Didn't get your bill paid on time? Accept it. Had a fight with your spouse over something insignificant? Accept it. Kids don't judge. One minute they are trying to run away from us because we are feeding them the medications, and the next, they are coming to us crying because their throat hurts. It isn't like they suffer from short-term memory loss and forget what you just tried to do to them. It is just that they don't judge. They don't see you for your flaws or "perfection". They don't see an enemy in you. They simply see a parent – their caretaker.

This is surely something we can learn from them!

Don't Hide From Your Emotions

Oh, the noises that come out of our children when they are mad or angry at us. Oh, how wide their mouths gape open when they are crying at the top of their lungs because they can't fit into the door's little opening for the cat. Yes, they can be dramatic, but they aren't afraid of their emotions and don't try to hide from them. Kids are expressive, and they are comfortable in letting others know what emotions they are going through. They know that feelings are important and, therefore, they mustn't be bottled up. They aren't ashamed of their feelings and rather quite open about them.

We should aim to be like kids too. Instead of bottling up our emotions, express them for our own sake. After all, we have all had those days when we cried our eyes out and felt immensely better after the emotional release. Remember how calm and light we felt instantly? As adults, we can learn appropriate ways to express our emotions in a way that is healthy, physically and emotionally, for us and those around us.

Forgive and Forget

The same kid who was just disciplined for misbehaving comes to you asking for help about something. Strange, but quite common, too! It is because kids rarely hold grudges towards their parents. They know how to let go and forgive someone for the mistakes they made. Everything seems to mend alright with a hug and kiss on the cheeks. They don't allow a harsh scolding ruin their whole day or week. We should do the same. We shouldn't let our emotions get the best of us and hold grudges with someone forever. We should learn to let go too and not let anything negative affect us for an extended period of time.

Curiosity Keeps Them Alive

It is as if they live for the thrill of the unknown. Children are always running around, poking their tiny hands into everything, peeking out of the windows, and asking a hundred questions about anything and everything. Their inquisitiveness is something we should learn from, as well. We should ask questions about the world around us. Why are things the way they are? How can we make the world a better place? What's the name of that mountain range to the north of us? Why and how do ocean tides work? We should be excellent researchers and pay close attention to all that's happening around us. After all, there is a whole wide world out there just waiting to be discovered!

Conclusion

We have come to the end of this book, which was aimed at delivering the values mindfulness practices hold. We hope that this has been a comforting journey for you, and that you feel much better about your parenting choice and willingness to make the requisite changes where necessary.

As parents, becoming mindful isn't something only we have to aspire to, it is something that we need to cultivate in our kids as well. And this has to start right now because we all know the fast-paced media and advertisers are all against us by keeping our kids fully engaged and distracted. Teaching mindfulness to kids enables their middle prefrontal cortex to grow. It is that part of our brains that regulates the body, strengthens willpower, creates emotional stability, incites empathy, morality, and promotes harmonious communication. Aren't all these characteristics you would want to see your kid grow up with?

We can help our kids achieve all this and much more if we start to model mindfulness ourselves. They are going to eventually follow in our footsteps when they notice the positive changes it brings into our lives, behaviors, and moods. One of the biggest problems we face today is the lack of presence of mind. We have introduced several worries into our lives deliberately. There is so much we stress over and get frustrated about without even realizing that the things we are angry over are not even in our control.

Therefore, what we need is acceptance, something we have talked about repeatedly in this book. The practices we introduce to our clients help them become more resilient against negative emotions and not let them become overpowering. When parents embody the practices of mindfulness, their children notice it, too. There have been cases where parents came back to thank us for familiarizing them with mindfulness as it helped them navigate through their emotions better and create a balance between their work and life.

Mindfulness teaches us to respond rather than react, but it also presents us with many ways to accept and cope with the emotions we feel when stressed out or frustrated. This prevents us from losing our sh*t, which has been the goal of the book since the beginning.

So pick up on the habits of mindful parenting and start acting responsibly and rationally. Below is a quick recap of all the things we have covered, so that you can refer to things quickly when you need a review of some of the main concepts we've discussed.

In the first chapter, we started with what frustration is, where it comes from and why we need to take care of our negative feelings. Later, we talked about the changes in parenting today and how it differs from parenting in earlier times.

In the second chapter, we introduced you to what mindfulness is all about, why is there such a hype about it, and if it is something that is going to help resolve the issues and challenges of parenting that modern-day parents have to deal with daily. Delving into the subject deeper, we looked at how a beginner can incorporate some of the most basic habits of mindfulness in their lives.

In chapter three, we talked about who kids are and how they are different from adults. We discussed the various personality types there are, and characteristics of each, to help parents determine the identity of their kids and deal with their distinct needs accordingly. In the second half of the chapter, we introduced you to what mindful listening is, what role it plays, and how you can practice this mindfulness technique with your children. To help parents get started, we ended the chapter with a few specific exercises to try.

Chapter four included a discussion on self-care, and how important it is to take care of ourselves, so that we can be mindful and present for those around us, especially our kids. Later, we discussed the different roles of a parent and how you shouldn't feel ashamed to seek advice and support from the people around you. There are many resources, including books, online forums, meetings and private counseling, to help you become the best person, and the best parent you can be.

In chapter five, we talked about what ownership of parenting means and how parents can become more aware of what their role is. We also discussed how some parents try to fix things quickly rather than be intentional with their actions and change a child's perspective about something rather than just correcting them.

In the final chapter, we discussed what being a role model to our kids' means and what trials it brings along with it. Then we introduced a unique but valuable way of looking at our own children, and children in general, as role models. There's so much we can learn from our "kids being kids," living in the moment, and taking it easy on ourselves.

With all that laid out, we hope that this book serves its purpose and makes your life as a parent a whole lot easier. Before we leave, remember that your goal shouldn't be to become a perfect parent, but simply a good one with positive values, ethics, and morals. When you demonstrate these, your kids will pick them up too without you ever trying to implement them. Aiming for perfection will only frustrate you further, as there will always be times when your kid acts out, misbehaves or disobeys orders. It is up to you and how you handle that.

Take a breath. Take things one moment at a time, and, finally...don't lose your sh*t!

Help Others Discover Mindful Parenting

Thank you for reading our book. We hope you enjoyed it as much as we enjoyed writing it. If you do enjoy this book and find it helpful in any ways, please consider leaving a review. Even just a few words will help others decide if the book is right for them.

We've made it super simple: just click the link below, and you'll travel to the Amazon review page for this book where you can leave your review.

Customer Reviews

There are no customer reviews yet.

More Ways to Practice Mindful Parenting

If you haven't done so, here's a chance to redeem the ultimate mindful parenting guide.

This checklist includes:

- 3 Techniques to mindfully deal with difficult situations.
- 11 Powerful phrases for mindful parenting.
- 15 Self-care strategies that will change your parenthood.

Visit this link: https://tinyurl.com/mindfulchecklist

References

Beach, S. R. (2014, October 21). Teaching Mindfulness to Teenagers: 5 Ways to Get Started. Retrieved from https://www.huffpost.com/entry/teaching-mindfulness-to-teenagers_b_5696247

Bean, S. (n.d.). 10 Things Parents Are Responsible For. Retrieved from https://www.empoweringparents.com/article/parenting-responsibilities-10-things-you-are-and-arent-responsible-for-as-a-parent/

Bethune, S. (2014, February 11). Retrieved from https://www.apa.org/news/press/releases/2014/02/teen-stress

Ceder, J. (2017, October 6). Mindful Parenting: How to Respond Instead of React. Retrieved from https://www.gottman.com/blog/mindful-parenting-how-to-respond-instead-of-react/

Duncan, L. G., Greenberg, M. T., & Coatsworth, J. D. (2009). Pilot Study to Gauge Acceptability of a Mindfulness-Based, Family-Focused Preventive Intervention. The Journal of Primary Prevention, 605–618.

Greenberg, D., & Ladge, J. J. (2019, November 5). How Being a Working Parent Changes as Children Grow Up. Retrieved from https://hbr.org/2019/09/how-being-a-working-parent-changes-as-children-grow-up

Hanceroglu, L. (2017). Retrieved from https://scholars.wlu.ca/cgi/viewcontent.cgi?article=3069&context=etd

Jaret, P., Bullock, G., Kuyken, W., Hunter, J., Sofer, O. J., & Newman, K. M. (2014, October 8). What is Mindfulness? Retrieved from https://www.mindful.org/what-is-mindfulness/

Kallus, J. (n.d.). HOW TO BECOME A MINDFUL PARENT. Retrieved from https://www.gaiam.com/blogs/discover/how-to-become-a-mindful-parent

Killingsworth, M. A., & Gilbert, D. T. (2010). A Wandering Mind Is an Unhappy Mind. Science, 932.

Lee, S.-L. (2020, February 19). Myers-Briggs: What's Your Child's Personality Type? Retrieved from https://www.figur8.net/2007/09/19/myers-briggs-childs-personality/

Lindberg, S. (2017, November 27). How to be a calmer parent. Retrieved from https://www.headspace.com/blog/2017/06/18/how-to-be-a-calmer-parent/

Marchand, W. (2012). Depression and Bipolar Disorder: Your Guide to Recovery. Boulder: Bull Publishing Company.

Marschel, L. (2019, May 28). Emotions Discovery Bottles Inspired By Disney's Inside Out. From Laly Mom: https://lalymom.com/emotions-discovery-bottles-inspired-by-disneys-inside-out/

Mindful Parenting. (n.d.). Retrieved from https://www.skillsyouneed.com/parent/mindful-parenting.html

Mrazek, M. D., Franklin, M. S., Phillips, D. T., Baird, B., & Schooler, J. W. (2013). Mindfulness Training Improves

Working Memory Capacity and GRE Performance While Reducing Mind Wandering. Psychological Science, 776–781.

Naumburg, C. (2013, January 27). What Is Mindful Parenting? Retrieved from https://www.huffpost.com/entry/mindful-parenting_b_2198097

Nichols, R. G., & Stevens, L. A. (1957, September). Listening to People. Harvard Business Review. Retrieved from https://hbr.org/1957/09/listening-to-people

O'Brian, M. (2019, August 28). What Is Mindfulness? (And What Does It Mean To You?) - Melli O'Brien. Retrieved from https://mrsmindfulness.com/what-is-mindfulness/

Rosas, L. (2017, December 22). Seeing The World Through The Eyes Of A Child. Retrieved from https://www.huffpost.com/entry/seeing-the-world-through-_b_13784800

Sanger, K. L., & Dorjee, D. (2015). Mindfulness training for adolescents: A neurodevelopmental perspective on investigating modifications in attention and emotion regulation using event-related brain potentials. Cognitive, affective & behavioral neuroscience, 696–711.

What Is Mindful Listening (and Seven Activities for Successful Listening)? (2020, January 15). Retrieved from https://www.developgoodhabits.com/mindful-listening/

Williams, V. (2015, April 23). Once Your Little Kids Are Big, Your Identity As A Parent Has To Change. Retrieved from https://www.mommyish.com/being-a-parent-of-older-kids/

www.ingramcontent.com/pod-product-compliance
Lightning Source LLC
Chambersburg PA
CBHW031049250726
48655CB00004B/1363